CHANGE (THE) MANAGEMENT

Change
Management
The

Why We as Leaders Must Change
for the Change to Last

Al Comeaux

LIONCREST
PUBLISHING

CHANGE (THE) MANAGEMENT

Why We as Leaders Must Change for the Change to Last

ISBN   978-1-5445-0916-7 *Hardcover*
   978-1-5445-0915-0 *Paperback*
   978-1-5445-0914-3 *Ebook*
   978-1-5445-0917-4 *Audiobook*

Library of Congress Control Number: 2020906370

To my greatest teachers: Harold, Adele, Katie, Charlotte and Courtney

Contents

Foreword 9

Introduction 13

Part One: We Are the Enemies of Change

1. This Is Not a "They" Problem 29

2. Enemy #1: Our Own Cognitive Dissonance 49

3. Enemy #2: Our Outdated Ideas About
   Communications 71

4. Enemy #3: We Let Inertia Get in the Way 95

5. Enemy #4: Our Belief in Change by Decree 117

6. Enemy #5: We Live in the Weeds 135

7. Enemy #6: How We View People 153

Part Two: How We Become the Allies of Change

8. Reorientation: We Pull. We Don't Push 169

9. We Align on the Problem 187

10. We Listen 205

11. We Model the Change 225

Conclusion: We All Have Choices 239

Acknowledgments 245

References 249

About the Author 263

Index 265

Foreword

By Terry Jones

I was wrapping up a consulting assignment a few years ago and having a final discussion with the CEO. We'd been working to help his organization change and adapt itself to this new all-digital world.

He and his division leaders seemed bought in and were actually leading the changes in their divisions. They weren't just giving speeches; they were doing it.

As I was leaving the meeting, the CEO said, "There's something that puzzles me. The changes and steps you helped us implement aren't new. They are the same ideas I had last year, but change didn't happen."

"Well," I replied, "how did you communicate the change you wanted?"

"By email," he said, softly.

As you will learn in this book, that is the crux of what is wrong with most efforts to change. Leaders think it can be accomplished with the push of a button and without actually having to change themselves.

In this insightful book, Al Comeaux gives numerous examples of how and why this happens, and more importantly, he *explains what to do about it.*

Al's thinking is influenced not only from being change-managed himself (like all of us inside organizations in the past three decades) but also from being an internal change agent and change leader all through his varied career. He's learned from successes and failures alike, and not many who opine on change management carry this kind of insider insight.

Al learned firsthand during the beginnings of Travelocity as we grew from a team of 12 to a 3,000-person public company with a $1 billion market cap.

As Travelocity was a startup growing up *inside* American Airlines and its subsidiary, Sabre, I knew we'd have to totally change the way we operated to succeed. But I had no idea how much.

Overcoming resistance from elsewhere in the company, we moved out of the corporate headquarters and brought disparate teams together to begin to build our own culture. And we brought in people from the outside who opened up new ways of thinking for existing employees.

Just as importantly, I realized I had to change if we were going to create a different way of thinking. The team needed a model, so I had to pull them through the change. Gone were the formal ways of communicating; our town halls consisted of me standing on someone's desk and talking about the latest achievement. It was communicating via action.

As Al says so insightfully, "For successful, enduring change... we have to pull."

He's right. We can't push change. We have to inspire it through our own actions. In short, we have to *pull*.

I've served on seventeen public and private boards, and led two public companies. I've spoken to tens of thousands of people around the world on innovation and change and written two books about it. Along the way, I've seen dozens of established firms fall by the wayside and only a few succeed in the wrenching and difficult process of change.

If you read Al's book and truly apply his lessons, perhaps you can actually lead the change your organization so badly needs in this period of extreme business disruption.

Terry Jones
Founder of Travelocity
Founding Chairman of Kayak
Author of *ON Innovation* and *Disruption OFF*

Introduction

Imagine for a minute a change management consultant pitching her services to an organization threatened by a competitor or new technology. She tells her audience that the changes they want are indeed achievable and that she has the best tools, training, and technology for the job. She shows an outstanding track record of ushering in successful, enduring change. She has a team of smart people who can come in and take names; they have all the technical, financial, and analytical models; and they can help paint the picture of the change in language that people will swoon for. People will *want* to change.

She has these executives eating out of her hand. They're impressed with her and gobsmacked by her results. Everyone in the room knows change initiatives are hard. Why not go with someone successful like this?

Then she leans on the conference room table to the rapt attention of the team and says, "You know, the one ingredient I don't have—but which I need—is a commitment from each of you to change. I need you to model the behaviors you're trying to drive throughout the organization. You want to drive a nimbler, more cost-efficient business, and this will only happen if you model nimbler and more cost-efficient behaviors yourselves. So you'll give up your assistants, and your people will see that you're keeping your own calendars and making your own copies and coffee. You'll give up your company cars and dedicated parking spaces; this will drive a shared 'we're in this together' attitude.

"You'll also need to approach the change differently from those you've done before—the ones that failed. Instead of deciding the change and foisting it on your people, you'll listen to your people to find out the best way to meet your goals. And you won't tell people to change; you'll ask them to come with you on the change journey. And before doing that, you'll work on your active listening skills and your meeting management skills. You guys keep scoring horribly in these areas on your engagement surveys."

People are frozen in place.

"Only with this kind of behavior from you—as leaders— can these other initiatives work," she continues. "Because most change management initiatives don't fail because the processes, training, and technology aren't right; they fail because people like you think you can change your organizations without the hard work of modeling the behavior you're calling for, leading the change and asking people to follow you. I will not work with you if you aren't willing to change your behaviors and attitudes. And before I'll even take this assignment, I want to interview each of you separately to understand if you're each capable of changing and whether the group dynamic can serve this change."

Everyone sits in stunned silence for a moment. Then they shift in discomfort. When the team starts to breathe normally again, they give the consultant a warm "Thank you" and send her on her way.

"We have to find someone just as successful who'll focus on the changes we actually need," someone says. "That jerk seemed to get distracted on nonessential things."

Everyone agrees.

A HUGE CHALLENGE

A massive change management industry has sprung up during the past three decades, and it sells managers on the idea that disciplined efforts to change the processes, technologies, and behaviors of frontline employees can be done with measurable management techniques that plan for and execute the change at hand.

I don't want to sell short what this industry does. Given that change is now constant—with some organizations having one or more firmwide changes per year—this is important work. Properly planning a technology cutover, moving to the cloud, prioritizing for the customer journey, changing the way we market and distribute our products, implementing new governance or safety policies, planning for a new work space, or merging organizations...these things can't be done without significant work, including assessing current capabilities, proper planning for how technology will be used, aligning project activities, understanding clearly how processes will be changed, analyzing cost and revenue and financial planning, and understanding how the necessary training will be delivered.

And, clearly, a fuller cultural renewal—a transformation with a brand-new way of thinking about the direction of the organization and the industry and even thinking about realigning the organization's values and mission—has to be a deliberate effort with consensus about what the future will look like, proven techniques, the right tools, and a roadmap to get there.

But according to a McKinsey & Company study, two-thirds of these efforts fail or fall far short of their goals. Something's amiss. If surgeons failed two-thirds of the time, there would be no confidence in the medical establishment. If a lawyer admitted to losing two-thirds of his trials, no one would hire him. But as perfectly adept leaders—often knowing full well that most change management efforts fail—we still sign up for these change efforts.

Given how much money and work goes into these efforts, that's a shame. Resources are wasted, the organization can lose focus, people's lives are upended, often with little to show for it. And with failure, the organization falls further behind the change curve.

So why do we keep trying? Are we masochists? Or are we optimists who simply believe we won't fail?

Usually, we don't have a choice in the matter. Globalization, changes in the marketplace, competitive pressures, changing customer expectations, threats like automation, and technologies like the internet, blockchain, and artificial intelligence all put tremendous pressure on organizations. As managers, we can't sit idly without trying to change how we do business. We have to try. But the efforts fail and fail again.

Why is this? Well, most of the literature on change management and most of the change management work and research has been done by academics and consultants—

people who've had a front-row seat to observe change efforts at many organizations. They've done great work and research—some of which I've used in this book—but it's largely missing a giant dimension of what's needed for full success.

In my thirty-plus-year career, I've spent four years in consulting and the rest mostly in leadership positions inside companies. In addition to my years leading communications and championing change at Travelocity, which was itself disrupting multiple industries at once, I've been on leadership teams at companies large and small, young and old, including American Airlines, GE, and Sabre. I can say beyond debate that there's a monumental difference between being inside and outside a company. I've been change-managed; consultants and tenured academics largely have not. I've gone to bed wondering if my company would exist the next day, thinking with my peers about how to flip our business model overnight. Consultants and academics aren't in the boat, paddling, taking on water. Their knowledge and observations are very useful to all of us, but I'm adding a needed dimension to it because—like you—I've been on the inside of this kind of change.

TAKE SMART, ADD HEART

To further defend these consultants, though, we need to

realize that our organizations demand that their change work be measurable. Management consultants have developed a strong framework for this, saying goals must be specific, measurable, achievable, relevant, and timely (SMART). We've all heard it: if you can't measure it, you can't manage it.

And the *results* must be measurable. The *inputs*, however, can't always be measured. If you've never been in the boat, been change-managed, you've never felt with all of your heart the unmeasurable power of certain things—certain inputs—that have actually changed your vigor and behavior as a worker. Without this insight, our focus is mostly on aspects of the intellect, not those of the heart.

But there is a way to succeed at change. As I've discovered and will share with you in this book, behavioral change— the very thing we need if changes are to last—requires emotional buy-in from those being asked to change their behaviors. Given the growing body of science pointing to the importance of emotion in decision-making—even in rational business decision-making—it's become clear that all the intellectual arguments and SMART work in the world will only drive so much change, and only for so long. For change management to work and last—for the energy to be there among those going through the change—we must focus on both the intellectual dimension and the emotional dimension: SMART *and* heart.

This is especially true when we address behavioral change. The reality is if we want successful, lasting change, we should *not* try to get people to change their behaviors. Trying to get people to change their behaviors is actually counterproductive. Instead, what we must do is to get people to *want* to change their behaviors. The former yields mere compliance; it'll last a while but usually not for long. The latter is contagious, energy-inducing, and lasting. And the difference is monumental.

The best way to drive a desire for behavior change—the best way to drive an emotional and intellectual connection during a change initiative—is for employees to understand the *what* and *why* of the change (rational connection) and to see examples of the change itself—*how* to change—from certain behaviors by leaders: modeling, listening, asking people to join, pulling people to the change (emotional connection). We leaders must have skin in the change.

It's a realization that's taken me twenty years to crystallize, and as you'll see throughout this book, it's something that will make change efforts richer and more successful.

MY EPIPHANY

How did I come to this certainty? Well, it started four companies ago. Actually, twenty years, four companies, eight jobs, eight CEOs, three CEO transitions, and countless other executive transitions, numerous corporate-wide and divisional change efforts (including an IPO, a hostile take-over, a take-private/leveraged buyout, two startups inside large corporations, massive globalization, and two 40 per-cent layoffs), working with scores of fellow executive-team peers, discussions with numerous management consul-tants and other senior executives, and thousands upon thousands of pages of reading ago.

It started in a conference room during training for a new job. I remember thinking for the first time ever, "Well, this job already sucks."

I had just moved a long way to join a leadership team in a corporate division, and my new boss, who led the divi-sion, had sent me to a course developed by Stephen Covey, *Principle-Centered Leadership*. I was a big fan of Covey's after reading and taking a course about his book *The 7 Habits of Highly Effective People*.

Given that we were about to embark on a division-wide change initiative with a whole new executive team, every-one else on the leadership team had already taken the class, and it was now being rolled out to other managers of people. The course included modules introducing the change ahead. As I had just joined the executive team, I needed to experience the course myself, so I joined the second class.

In advance of the course, I heard our HR leader encourage our boss to speak to this second class. "You should encourage the participants to throw themselves into it," the HR leader said, "given that you recently took the course yourself."

The leader, a reserved fellow, was very reluctant. "You know I'm not into that touchy-feely stuff," the boss said.

I began to wonder if the course was the boss's idea or the HR leader's. The HR leader finally talked the boss into speaking to the class, but it did more harm than good.

When the boss got up to speak, he bombed. You could tell his heart wasn't into what he was saying. Not only did he not model the change, but his body language hardly showed support for it. And therefore, it didn't resonate with the class.

These were mostly middle or frontline managers—the people we needed most for the change initiative to succeed. It became clear during the rest of the course that our change initiative was already on thin ice; my classmates used our leader's milquetoast performance as a cue that this wasn't a serious effort. They disengaged or openly scoffed at everything being taught.

For me, the problem ran deeper: I would have to communicate about this change program. Why the new ways of doing things would be better. Why a new way of thinking was going to help us improve. The leader, my boss, would expect my communications to get people to feel and think differently. A new day was dawning, and they needed to experience it through communications, as much or more than through any other way. Or so he expected.

So I went to work. We developed whole new platforms for communicating with the team, and the team received them politely. But I had to admit to myself—and my peers on the leadership team had to admit to themselves—that this was window dressing. The boss wasn't modeling the change. And though we tried, there was no real measurement to our program—positive or negative—so the program ended up being good PR for our leader, who shared this work with his higher-ups, but it left us in the same boat as before.

He got a promotion. I got a two-year lesson in how *not* to do change management, transformation, or reengineering. "But," I wondered, "what's the right way?"

SO MANY SIMILAR EXAMPLES

In my conversations during the next twenty years with scores of senior executives at other organizations, and with management consultants who focus on change issues, I've found a tragic number of examples like this.

The organization sets out to transform itself, but it can't. Senior managers eventually blame middle management for failing to lead the change. But ultimately, after some digging—and often some sheepish admission on the part of some of these executives—I find what's really gone on is that those who are honest with themselves know that senior leadership didn't walk the talk. These leaders can't or won't model the change, and therefore, the people expected to change have no one to follow. They have no one modeling the new behavior, the new way.

Some of these executives (I would call them less self-aware or less honest if I'm being, well, honest) start by saying something like, "We couldn't get our people to change. They had been doing things a certain way for so long, and then we needed them to do things differently, to think differently, to act differently. They couldn't handle it."

I asked one of these execs a rather impolite question (or so I gathered from the look on his face): "So did *you* have to change, or was it really your people who had to change?"

"No, it was our people," he said, his voice getting louder. "They couldn't change. We painted this great vision for them. They were excited about it. But we just don't have the kind of people who are capable of the kind of change we needed."

Honestly, after all I had learned from so many others, I wanted to hold up a mirror to this guy.

WHAT I'VE LEARNED

In fact, what I've learned, and what I'm certain of is this: having leaders who model change is by no means the only important factor in successful change efforts. But *not* having leaders who truly support and model the change—or worse, having leaders who act incongruently or in any way unsupportive—has to be the single biggest factor in change efforts that fail.

So many things can go wrong in a change. This one thing must go right.

And according to McKinsey & Company, the large majority of failed changes result from either management's failure to show support for the change or employees' resistance to the change. And resistance to change—as we'll see—can be overcome when managers truly support the change. So these are two sides of the same coin.

As an insider leading change and being changed, some of the worst moments of my career have been times when leaders wouldn't walk the talk...when they foisted the change on employees and expected radically different outcomes. And yet, some of the very richest moments of my career—and clearly the lynchpins of successful and enduring changes I've seen, the times when I've *wanted* to change, the times when I found the energy to change even when I was tied down with so many other things on my plate—have been when leaders have modeled the change they've wanted from employees. (I'll share a few of those stories with you.)

By their actions, they've taught me how to do it, and they and the many other model leaders I've researched have inspired me to share this book, poring over the research to explain some very simple—but very hard—things that I think must be heard and understood by leaders at all levels in all kinds of organizations.

I've also written this for personal reasons. In just a decade, my own children will be in the workforce, and I want their chosen institutions to still be around and strong. I also realize, given the estimated $3 trillion to be spent on change each year—meaning $2 trillion is wasted on unsuccessful change—that if my work can improve the success rate by just 1 percent, I can have a hand in helping businesses avoid wasting $20 billion. And if the success rate improves, it will mean that the work and pain endured by thousands or millions of employees and their leaders won't have been done in vain.

Today's organizations cannot be complacent. Change used to be a one-off; it's now continuous.

Part One

We Are the Enemies of Change

ONE

This Is Not a "They" Problem

Theyak. Theyakness.

These aren't words. I've simply substituted T-H-E-Y for the letters that should be there: W-E. (If spelled correctly, they would be "weak" and "weakness.")

We're often guilty of saying that problems with change programs are "they" problems. But these start as "we" problems. Our habit of putting "they" in places that should have "we" is, well, a weakness on our part.

In fact, the dirty secret I've come to understand—and the problem we need to solve together in this book—is that we are the enemies of change. (This includes me...guilty as charged.) We take every opportunity—consciously or subconsciously—to get in change's way. We miss the need for change in the first place because of the successes we've had. We try shortcuts that can do more harm than good. Our beliefs are rooted in the 1970s, and we don't realize how outdated they are. And we blame things on others... on "they."

We need to change if we want anyone else to change. And we can.

THE WE-ATTITUDES

Moving from *They Attitudes* to *We Attitudes*

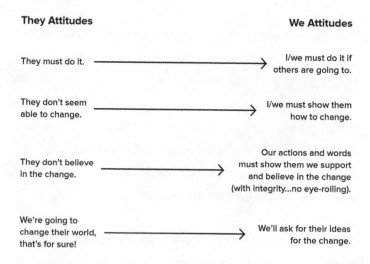

They Attitudes
We Attitudes

They must do it. → I/we must do it if others are going to.

They don't seem able to change. → I/we must show them how to change.

They don't believe in the change. → Our actions and words must show them we support and believe in the change (with integrity...no eye-rolling).

We're going to change their world, that's for sure! → We'll ask for their ideas for the change.

Change can face a lot of challenges—challenges we'll discuss in the next six chapters and beyond—and people like you and me create many of them. Anyone, really, who leads people at any level in an organization can frustrate change. But we don't always understand how, we don't necessarily see that we're doing it even when we're doing it, and we aren't always aware that our own natures are working against us. (I'll share examples in the next few chapters.) We must recognize that the problem with change starts with "we," not "they."

WHEN SENIOR LEADERS POINT TO "THEY"

Of all my discussions and reading and experiences in search for the right way to do change management, the pivotal one—the one that shaped my thesis before further research—came when I ran into a senior executive at a highly respected consumer-facing company headquartered in the Midwest. We met at a conference we both attended each year.

This was about 2006, and his company was facing an existential threat called the internet. I had spent five years disrupting the storefront travel agent industry—among other industries—while at Travelocity, so I wondered how a company like his would go about fighting something as disruptive as the internet. They were indeed deep into a change management effort that would reset the very direction of their company.

"Change management? What *is* that, exactly?" I asked him.

Honestly, I had heard this buzzword countless times, but no one seemed to be talking about the same thing when they used terms like this.

"Well, we're having to look at everything we do and think about it differently," he said. He explained the threat they'd identified, the processes and technologies they would need, and the metrics they had developed as an executive team. They had reached consensus together as a team on what success would look like. His CEO had begun communicating to the company about exactly what they would become—what the company would look like in the future. They would be nimbler, they would be bolder with bigger ideas. They wouldn't be so risk-averse. And they had goals and champions and ambassadors for all of the work they were doing. People were excited, ready for the change, he said.

This guy had explained the concept of change management more succinctly and passionately than most.

When I ran into him during a break at the same event a year later, I asked him how his company's change efforts were going. His smiling face went flush. "It's slow," he said, sounding disheartened. "We still have a lot of work ahead of us. We've had so much success over the last one hundred years doing things a certain way. People are used to getting gold stars for doing things the old way, and that's hard to overcome."

We ran out of time, but that evening, I caught up with him at the bar to continue our conversation.

"You know," he said to me, "I was so excited about this change management work when you and I talked last year. It was so obvious we needed to do it. We laid out a great vision as an executive team. But it's actually been a mess. What it comes down to, really, is that the leaders aren't able to change. I mean, some of the leaders actually did change, and their people followed. But there were only a few of us. Most of the senior managers talked a good game and repeated back what the CEO was saying, but they just couldn't get their heads around the idea that *they* actually needed to change themselves. They weren't acting any differently. Many wondered why *their* people weren't changing.

"Others were cynical about it; they've survived change initiatives before, and they just thought they needed to outlast this one, like in the past.

"The CEO recognized who was capable of change and held them up as success stories. But that brought a backlash from the rest of the crew. So now, I think—I hope—the CEO is in the process of changing out the leaders who haven't been able to model the change.

"But it's hard. You have an executive who's been a superstar for twenty-five years, knocking her numbers out of the park. She's been promoted umpteen times; she's been recognized as a great leader. But that was all in the old world. How does the CEO suddenly come in and say, 'You, the person I thought might be my successor, you don't belong here anymore'?

"It's really tough for him, and I'm worried he won't end up being able to make those kinds of moves. If he can't make the changes, the whole effort will basically fall apart."

Over the next few years, I watched this company. The CEO eventually announced a number of major senior personnel changes, and fortunately, things did turn around well—eventually—but not before this hundred-year-old company was changed, whether its leaders liked it or not.

Forget change management. Management was changing.

The reality is we can all come up with reasons why "they" need to change and "we" don't. We can point the finger at middle management, at other companies, at bigger projects that need it more than ours, at the lowliness of our own positions, and even at other industries affecting ours. But only "we" hold our futures in our hands; "they" do not.

NOT MY ORGANIZATION

Let's take the idea that other companies are the "they" that need to change (not "us"). For example, some of us may think a book about change management is primarily for large, complex organizations going through radical change. The reality is, the lessons here can apply to many kinds of organizations, companies or not. And I got proof of this while I was writing this book.

I was having breakfast with a lifelong friend, I'll call him Michael, who was the managing partner at a law firm of about thirty attorneys. I was telling him about the need for corporate leaders to model the change their businesses need, how it makes total sense but it's not common practice. I was sharing some big corporate examples.

He listened to what I was saying. At first—he admitted later—he was thinking this didn't apply to him. Then he started to look at me a bit sheepishly. "That's like my firm," he said. "We just got audited by one of our biggest clients, a huge multinational insurance company that we do a lot of work for. They told us we had great systems and processes, but we don't use them. They expect us to use them going forward.

"Well," he said, "I walked back into my office after the meeting, and there was paper everywhere. I like to print everything out, insurance policies, legal memoranda, all kinds of things. If I need to cross-reference things, I can have two documents open at the same time on my desk or my lap. The client thinks I should use two or three screens to multitask, but that's not how I learned to do things. I remember thinking, I'm hopeless.

"Now that I think about it, when I walk by some of the other offices, the younger attorneys are almost as bad as me. Some are worse. Now that I hear what you're saying, I guess I know where they're getting permission for this and why they don't think they need to change. I guess if the boss doesn't do it, they don't need to do it."

Michael left that firm for another shortly after the day we had breakfast, and he used the occasion to start fresh. He (claims he) now is adept at using the systems that his client insisted on, and he expects it of the other lawyers, especially those who went with him to the new firm.

The reality is this can apply to any organization of any kind, any size, and any type. Nonprofits, government organizations, schools, police forces, mom-and-pops, and, yes, my good friend's law firm.

"We" is a wide net.

MY CHANGE ISN'T BIG ENOUGH

Another "they" people point to are those who are having massive turnaround efforts. "Our" change isn't big enough to model.

Not every change an organization undertakes will be transformational or done to hold off an existential threat. Many of us just want to establish a new process or capability. That doesn't mean these lessons don't apply to "us."

While writing this book, I was having a beer with another lawyer friend of mine (I'll call him Ross) who is corporate secretary for a Fortune 300 company. He was listening to my explanation and said, "You know, I'm trying to implement a new compliance process for approval protocols. It's very important that we start acting like a real company and do these kinds of things right. But it's not the kind of transformational change that you're talking about. How would someone model a compliance protocol?"

In reality, not every change is worthy of what we normally think of as modeling. "But," I said, "every change—no matter the size—needs two things that equate to modeling: leaders who will support the change and leaders who will act congruently with the change."

We can't have leaders who hear the word "compliance" and roll their eyes. They can't say, "Oh, yeah, what a pain all this compliance stuff is. I'll never get my real work done." They have to genuinely support it, or their teams will value it as little as they do.

We also can't have leaders—even if vocally supportive—

who ignore the new protocol. They have to act consistently with the change as it's called for.

I caught my friend, Ross, reflecting on this later in the conversation, as he thought through the leaders he would need for his change to be successful. He had already determined where to start building support, and he was thinking about how he would ask certain people if he could count on them to support it fully themselves and in front of their teams. He also was thinking of how he could impress upon these same leaders to break old habits and act in line with the new protocols.

"We" is in all kinds of places in our organizations.

THEY DON'T HAVE TO CHANGE

Then there's the idea that our people *have* to change; they have no choice. In reality, they don't really have to change even if we're demanding it.

For the third time in my career, an organization where I worked was planning a significant internal transformation in its IT processes—from waterfall to agile. Historically, the IT organization would get its marching orders from its internal customer and go off and build a capability, then they'd come back months later and often find out that—through a misunderstanding—they had built a core part of the capability incorrectly. This linear, sequential practice in which a second project starts only after the previous project is completed and approved is called "waterfall development."

We were moving to agile development, where developers instead take on a small amount of work for a two-week sprint and come back to their internal customer to make sure they've gotten it right.

Compared to waterfall's months-long cycles, agile requires a much more prescriptive work process, often with exercises like morning standup meetings that keep each individual accountable on a daily basis for meeting the requirements of the sprint. Many organizations have moved to agile, and many more have attempted it.

An acquaintance from IT who was working on the change was mentioning it to me, and—having seen things work better in some places than others—I asked her, "How will we get people to *want* to make the change?"

"Well," she paused, the question stopping her in her tracks, "they have to." I could sense an unspoken "of course" to her answer.

That's an outdated understanding of things. There's Glassdoor.com, LinkedIn, Indeed.com, ZipRecruiter, and many other places these professionals can go to instead of participating in the change. They can also resist from inside.

There's a saying in football: "It's not the Xs and Os, it's the Jimmys and Joes." It's not about having the best plays on our white board; it's about recruiting and retaining the best players we can. Even in rough financial times, when candidates are aplenty, we're still in a war for the very best talent.

So I said, "You know, they don't really have to do it. They can get other jobs. I'm sure there are other places still doing things the old way. Maybe some of these people even decided to work here because they prefer waterfall. Let me help you think through what's going to get them to *want* to stay and become agile developers."

She let me in. We partnered. We impressed on others in the organization the importance of *showing* support by using ourselves as examples. And we got senior members of the IT leadership team to take time out of their busy schedules to train others in agile development and to be mentors to the teams in the first few sprints.

Some people still left, but several years later, agile had become the only way to do development in this organization. It was embraced throughout the organization, and it has improved costs, efficiency, and working relationships between IT and its internal customers.

THE HIGHER-UPS ARE THE "THEY"

When we're coming up through the ranks, we may say the "they" is the CEO and other leaders. "But I'm not the CEO," we might say. "I can't make any of this change happen." Well, we're going to spend most of this book exploring how leaders of people, including executive teams, are the "we" that need to change—the people who need to model change. But I would be remiss if I allowed any of us to cop out on our ability to be change agents. None of us is off the hook here.

Let me share a couple of stories—one of my own, one I've seen elsewhere—that are testimony to the fact that anyone anywhere in the organization can successfully lead a change effort that sticks.

WHEN MARTIN WORKED THE MATRIX

A somewhat junior employee in my organization (I'll call him Martin) was a change agent. I supported him and his efforts as much as I could, but he sometimes couldn't let things go. When I told him something wouldn't work, he often kept coming at me about it.

One time, Martin was having trouble getting through to me about an idea he had for a video communications capability. This was 2005, and I kept telling Martin that our IT team had made it clear that our current platform couldn't handle much video content without overtaxing the system, potentially bringing the system down.

He scheduled a meeting on my calendar, but it was about the video topic, which he wouldn't let go of, so I was debating whether to attend. He predicted this, and the evening before, as we were both wrapping things up, he came into my office to get me to commit to attend. He had a number of outside people coming in for the meeting and didn't want to let them down, given that some were flying in. He promised it would be worth my time. I agreed to attend.

When I walked into the conference room, I had an experience that completely opened me up. He had booked a conference room large enough that he could put the tables in a horseshoe; it suddenly dawned on me that he probably had to reserve the room weeks in advance, given how much this particular conference room was in demand. Each seat had a name tent with a name already written on it. There were materials nicely put together for each participant at their seat. There were even two name tents for people from IT—the very people who had told me we couldn't funnel video through the current pipes. Turns out, Martin had already briefed them on this technology.

Across from me sat the CEO of the company that was offering this new software. He and his team seemed impressive. Given that Martin had now told me—through his actions—

that *this is important*, my mindset had completely flipped. I was now ready to listen.

Clearly, Martin had properly briefed the outside team, and it took them no time to get me to understand what they were selling and why it was a good thing for our business, as well as how it would get around our IT capacity issues. The IT people confirmed this; in fact, this new capability solved several additional problems for them—and saved them money.

Martin had found this firm, learned all he could, built coalitions in the organization, refused to listen to my naysaying, and had singlehandedly willed this technology to installation. He had gotten me to *want* to change. He did it through my sense of sight—stopping me in my tracks by making it impossible to ignore his preparation throughout the room. When I went to explain this capability to my CEO, I, of course, took Martin with me, so he could give the pitch.

The video capability became an enabler of other global changes that "we" (senior management) could drive through a new communications platform.

And if this junior person can drive change this way and you can't, well, maybe you aren't as passionate as Martin was. Remember, you, too, are "we." And "we" (senior management) need to get hit over the head (softly!) every once in a while if we're going to change.

THE SMELL OF GLOVES

John Stegner was no CEO either. He was a purchasing employee at a large manufacturer, and he recognized that there was huge opportunity to save costs by consolidating the purchasing process, which at the time was owned by each division.

In *The Heart of Change* by John Kotter and Dan Cohen, John Stegner says, "I thought we had an opportunity to drive down purchasing costs not by 2 percent but by something on the order of $1 billion over the next five years." It didn't matter that he wasn't CEO; what he was, was determined. He asked a summer intern to research just one item purchased throughout the organization—gloves. He figured he could use gloves as a proxy for purchasing overall.

The intern found out that the company was purchasing 424 different types of gloves. Two different plants bought the same exact pair of gloves, with one plant paying $5 and the other paying $17.

Stegner could have provided this information in a Power-Point presentation or on a spreadsheet. Instead he asked the intern to collect all 424 glove types and label them by plant and price. Once he had the gloves, he invited all of the division presidents to take a look at what he and the intern had found. The gloves were all piled up on the usually pristine boardroom table.

"They looked at two gloves that seemed exactly alike, yet one was marked $3.22 and the other $10.55. It's a rare event when these people don't have anything to say. But that day, they just stood with their mouths gaping," he said.

When they did speak, they asked, "We really buy all these different kinds of gloves?"

Yes, they did.

I would have loved to have been there that day. Not to see the looks on the faces of the division presidents—although that would have been interesting—but to see, feel, and smell the pile of gloves. If you want to make a powerful impact on people, find a simple sensory way to do it.

As we'll see when we talk about the New York subway system, as we saw with Martin, and as we see with these gloves on the usually pristine boardroom table, appealing to the senses of others—in a nonthreatening way—can move people when they otherwise might not be willing to listen or act. It drives an emotional response that PowerPoints and spreadsheets and nagging our bosses and discussions at meetings just can't do.

In Stegner's case, the division presidents were so impressed with what they learned that they asked him to take the glove display on the road and share it throughout the divisions.

The organization eventually consolidated purchasing, saving hundreds of millions of dollars.

But imagine if Stegner's mindset was about "they." What if he thought he wasn't powerful enough to build support for a change like this? And imagine if he had tried only to communicate through the rational, not the emotional—taking a PowerPoint presentation from conference room to conference room. They'd likely still be getting ripped off on gloves and who knows what else.

BOTTOM LINE

If you want change, it can't be about "they." We all have a responsibility to drive it, especially the "we" called senior management. And we have to do it by modeling it, by reaching people on an emotional level. We hear the phrase "walk the talk," and in many ways, that's what I'm talking about here. But walking the talk isn't easy.

So in the remainder of Part One, we'll look at how our own actions and/or lack of awareness can frustrate change or even stop change in its tracks. This is about building self-awareness so we can identify these frustrations and stop ourselves when these things are happening.

Once we're off the backs of our heels, so to speak, we then explore what it takes to succeed at change, including modeling, listening, and pulling our people towards the change. Part Two explores what we need to understand and how we can go about transforming our organizations by modeling the change we want to see. This gives us a working formula that can help in any kind of change.

Let's get started.

CHAPTER ONE

Chapter 1 is tough on us...on anyone who leads people and wants to lead change.

- We are the enemies of change.
- We often think our challenges for change programs are "they" problems, such as problems with middle management or front line employees.
- When assessing the biggest challenges to change, we need to look at ourselves first.
- We take every opportunity—conscious or unconscious— to get in change's way.
- We also are enemies of change when we think the organizations where we work, the projects we work on, the people who work for us, and the positions we hold make the change a "they" thing, not a "we" thing.

TWO

Enemy #1

Our Own Cognitive Dissonance

I was recently at a gathering of financial health professionals—people who want to help those who can't get credit easily, people who want to improve the financial lives of the underserved.

Speaking at this event was Kai Ryssdal, the host of the very popular *Marketplace* on public radio. Public radio...people focused on the financially underserved...you get the sense this meeting did not attract many conservatives.

Ryssdal talked about the need for people on both ends of the political spectrum to hear and listen to what the other side is saying. So he asked the group of about 300 if they could raise their hands if anyone had ever watched a full hour of prime-time Fox News.

Most of the audience groaned, and perhaps three hands went up—one was his.

His point is that we have to listen to other ideas, or we'll soon be toast as a country. My point is that we don't want to, and it's because of something called cognitive dissonance.

WHAT IS COGNITIVE DISSONANCE?

Cognitive dissonance is the feeling of psychological discomfort we get when a value or belief we hold as settled in our minds comes into question. Millions of people try to avoid cognitive dissonance every weeknight by turning on MSNBC if they're politically liberal or Fox News if they're conservative. What we all want is affirmation of our beliefs or our outlook. We're comfortable with the way we think; our day is easy when the things that usually happen, happen again.

The theory of cognitive dissonance was developed at the University of Minnesota in the 1950s by Leon Festinger, a pioneer in several areas of psychology whose hypothesis has spurred more than sixty years of further thinking and experimentation in social psychology.

He posited that a smoker who very much enjoys the practice but hears that smoking is unhealthy will have dissonance in his thinking if he continues to smoke, and he'll look for a way to resolve this dissonance. He can quit smoking. Or he can tell himself that smoking keeps his weight down, helps keep his thinking sharp, or is just worth continuing, given the relaxation and enjoyment he gets from doing it. Either way—accepting the information and acting on it, or finding ways to continue to act in the same manner without the dissonance in our head—we naturally want to avoid the feeling of cognitive dissonance. We don't like being wrong.

The same can be true in our business lives. We think that the way we act, how we relate to others, the attitudes we carry, the beliefs we have about how things should work and whether *we* need to change—all of these are normal.

And our normal only gets more cemented in us when we get positive feedback about these things. In our work life, we get compliments, "attagirls," promotions, raises. This tells us that our normal is the right kind of normal—it's the norm. We can't shake our beliefs about the way things are, given how often these values have been reinforced.

If someone challenges a deeply held belief, the dissonance can make us angry, it can make us withdraw, and we can go into denial about it. We tell ourselves this person is wrong because we've been successful, and our organization has been successful doing things a certain way with a certain attitude, treating people a certain way, thinking of things a certain way.

This can be hardest on executives. We executives have reached the summit. We're most likely the strongest believers in our normal as *the* normal. We've been told, not only in words but in actions, that our natural ways and the habits we've developed are the right ones.

We don't like ideas that actually challenge our values. So we try to get rid of them—by ignoring them, by finding a way to reaffirm our own beliefs, or developing an altogether new belief. We'll do very counterproductive things to hold on to our values.

ONE EXAMPLE: DISK DRIVE MAKERS

This idea of clinging to our value systems even when it's shown to be counterproductive was made clear in Clayton Christensen's classic business book *The Innovator's Dilemma*. Christensen retells the story of the computer disk drive industry in the early days of commercial computing to show how perfectly smart and disciplined managers can run businesses into the ground (one generation after another) without realizing it until it's too late.

He chose to study the disk drive industry for the same reason geneticists study fruit flies. If geneticists were to study humans, they would get a new generation only every thirty years or so; with fruit flies, a friend told him, there's a new generation every day. For business research, the disk drive industry of the 1970s and 1980s was perfect to study, given the birth-to-death cycle those organizations went through again and again.

When IBM invented the first computer disk, it was two feet in diameter. The company's engineers developed a drive apparatus the size of a large kitchen appliance that incorporated fifty of the disks, enough to store five megabytes of data. Technology improved, and new entrants sprung up with smaller disk drives that could hold greater capacity.

The fourteen-inch disk drive eventually became the industry standard in mainframe computers, and the makers of the fourteen-inch drive became chieftains of the industry.

The fact that new entrants were working on eight-inch disk drives didn't matter to these very smart executives who were busy taking orders for their fourteen-inch drives. Their mainframe customers specifically told them they didn't want the eight-inch drives, with their inferior capacity and higher costs. Christensen rightly argues that these leaders made rational decisions based on the data they had, and this data—including convincing demands from customers—told the executives to keep investing in better and better fourteen-inch drives.

Eventually, however, the eight-inch drives found a market: minicomputers. Minicomputer manufacturers were more focused on size and—in the near term—less focused on costs and capacity. Once these new entrants had the resources to further develop their eight-inch drives, they developed innovations to improve capacity and lower unit costs, eventually surpassing what even mainframe manufacturers were demanding.

Customers—including mainframe manufacturers who had initially shown no interest in eight-inch drives—abandoned the fourteen-inch drives for the eight-inch competitors. For the makers of fourteen-inch drives—even the few who eventually developed an eight-inch drive—it was too late. They all exited the market.

Now the eight-inch drive was dominant. Revenues were building and profits were rolling in. How would these manufacturers deal with 5.25-inch disk drives being developed at new startups? Engineers at some of the eight-inch drive manufacturers saw this as a threat and developed their own 5.25-inch drives. But ultimately, eight-inch makers largely ignored this market, even though they had developed their own eight-inch drives when the market for those drives was small and their technology was inferior. Then the 5.25-inch disk drive found a market: desktop personal computers, and the same thing happened all over again.

New entrants began developing 3.5-inch drives, and the process repeated itself once more, with these drive makers finding a market—laptops—and the 5.25-inch drive makers making the same mistakes. And so on.

You have to believe someone somewhere at or around these organizations warned these executives about the perils of repeating the same mistakes as the previous generations of makers. In fact, according to Christensen, who interviewed executives at many of these companies for his 1997 book, the warnings started when engineers at the eight-inch disk drive manufacturers saw and acted on the 5.25-inch threat—but to no avail.

As Christensen says, "Their managers either ignored [the principles of disruptive innovation] or chose to fight them."

These leaders had to be reconciling cognitive dissonance by rationalizing away any threat from the next set of new entrants, saying, "Our customers don't want or need them," and "Revenue projections are very slim for the 3.5-inch market."

In hindsight, this could be seen as rational thinking. In some of these cases, it took years for the next generation of disk drive to overtake the incumbents—the frogs being boiled alive slowly. But we have to think in foresight, not hindsight, using the lessons we have. And there were enough history lessons in these cases—their own histories, even—to teach them they should watch out, yet they didn't. They'd seen other frogs get boiled—they'd even lit the match on the stove—but thanks to cognitive dissonance, they failed to see themselves in the same light.

HOW IT AFFECTS CHANGE

Cognitive dissonance is an enemy of change—on multiple levels.

For individual contributors, cognitive dissonance hampers their ability to do things a different way because "this is the way we've always done it." Their language, their approach to problem-solving, so many things they draw upon each day, are tied to the existing way.

For executives, it's even worse. One of our long-held beliefs as leaders—a value of ours, even if outdated—is now that we've reached higher levels in our organization, we're strategists: we don't get involved in the day-to-day management of things. We paint the picture; we only clear the path for change. (And truth be told, we shouldn't micromanage.)

But we get cognitive dissonance when we hear that we have to get our hands dirty by modeling change. In fact, we actually doom change when we don't accept that our every action will be looked at by our people to determine if we're serious about the change.

Given that our people are suffering from cognitive dissonance themselves as they go through the difficult changes we expect of them, they're looking for their own exits. They want to deny that this change is necessary. They're looking to comfort themselves with any sign that tells them they don't really have to suffer through this change.

What's the very best evidence that tells them this change isn't for real? Signs that it's not a serious effort. And the best sign—the clearest signal—that's it's not serious, is the slightest evidence that leaders aren't bought in. And the best sign that leaders aren't bought in is if these leaders do things incongruent with the change. "Aha," these employees say consciously or subconsciously, "the leaders aren't serious about this. Good news. I can go back to my old way of thinking."

THE $1 FARE TO FIJI

This very well could have happened when a massive change being attempted at Travelocity was threatened by a simple technical snag.

In fact, something tells me Michelle Peluso already fully understood the concept of cognitive dissonance and the value of congruent action when, as the relatively new CEO at Travelocity, she awoke one day to find out that—due to a data glitch—a $1 fare from Los Angeles to Fiji had been on the website for some time. Compounding this, someone on a frequent flyer message board had noticed the fare and broadcast it to everyone reading the board. Lots of people were booking flights to Fiji from LA. Media who monitored the message board contacted Travelocity, alerting Michelle and the team.

The team quickly corrected the fare and set up better monitoring systems and processes to ensure this didn't happen again—or if it did happen somehow, they could catch it quickly.

Meanwhile, a debate ensued as journalists covered the topic. Should customers really be able to claim the fare when they obviously knew it was a mistake? United Airlines had recently said no on a cheap fare to Paris that had shown up on its website, and the airline had been skewered.

But, as we'll see, for Michelle and the team at Travelocity, there was much more at stake than a skewering: they were about to usher in a major change that could easily be undermined by how they reacted to this Fijian dollar fiasco.

Let's go back about eighteen months to when I led communications and was championing change at Travelocity. For some time, we had been wondering amongst ourselves how we could differentiate our brand, our offering. Price was driving consumer behavior, and we needed to be different, we needed to bring more value to the consumer.

At one point, a creative agency recommended as an aside that Travelocity could differentiate itself by offering a customer guarantee. The agency recommended a book called *Extraordinary Guarantees* and offered to introduce the author. I remembered this comment later and purchased the book, read it, and got hooked on the idea. I bought ten more books, handed them out to other leaders, begged them to read it, and the idea took off.

The concept of a guarantee is to differentiate yourself with consumers, improve quality, and save money at the same time. By putting your back against the wall with a guarantee, you can no longer afford to drop the ball, so in preparation, you build the systems and processes you need, and you create the training needed to absolutely keep your business on track. It's not for the faint of heart; if you fail, your business can go right down with it.

Let's say a customer calls in on Friday night with kids screaming because their hotel's pool is broken. Preguarantee, we would either disappoint the customer with no change in hotels, or a customer service representative would call around to find another hotel of the same quality—draining resources. This happened often, even for the same problem at the same hotel.

Now, new software would change the way we thought about—and how we worked—the Friday-night-screaming-kid-broken-pool issue. Agents got free rein to book an even nicer hotel because—thanks to the customer's call and a call to the hotel to find out what was going on there—we now knew to trigger the software. It automatically emailed every customer who had a future booking at that hotel, alerted them that the pool would be broken until at least a certain date, and offered them several other nearby hotels that they could book online right away for no extra charge. This delighted the future guests, eliminated future calls about the same hotel, lightened the load of our agents, solved current guests' problems much faster, and saved significant staff time—leading to lower costs and better margins.

So Michelle and the team were sold on the guarantee and what it could do to differentiate Travelocity while improving service and lowering costs.

The problem was that call center staff didn't believe we could possibly be serious about all of this. This was going to be change for them—a change in policies, procedures, and technology—so, thanks to cognitive dissonance, they were looking for a reason not to buy in. And, truth was, we hadn't always invested in our call centers as much as we could have. Some of our previous call center leaders had been old-school, "numbers-only-please" people. Agents hadn't felt the love.

Given that I led communications—and based on my excitement—I went out to our call centers a couple months before the launch to announce the guarantee, socialize it with leaders, and evangelize it to agents. We called this effort "customer championship," with a presentation entitled "Are You a Champion?"

I got a lot of stares and almost no questions. Clearly, we were disconnected from the reality the agents had faced, and they were crossing their arms in disbelief that things would change.

At that point, I had cognitive dissonance. The guarantee was going to be a *great* thing for our business. A giant change in how we did business—something I had personally championed in its earliest days—had taken flight. Although it actually started with an ad agency, I felt like I had birthed it, and others had taken my baby of an idea and believed in it so much—reinforced my rightness so much—that they had raised it to adolescence, invested millions of dollars and eighteen months getting buy-in from many groups, testing it with consumers, and building the excitement to a fever pitch. Now it was ready for adulthood. Everyone who had worked on it was sold on the idea. How could anyone have beliefs different from mine?

But they did. It was like a punch to the stomach, and I salved my dissonance by telling myself how wrong they were, even as I had the same experience at each call center. I was disheartened and also searching for a way to help others understand what was at play. So I went back to our main office and shared this with peers, including Michelle. The cognitive dissonance spread.

I met with our training team and told them to be ready for this when they went out to the call centers, and they revised the training to take this into account. But by the end of training, the agents still were in wait-and-see mode at best. We were all on pins and needles.

Then, at what seemed like the worst possible time, just a few days before the guarantee was to be launched, Fiji Airways and its $1 fare popped up. You could imagine what agents were saying: "Here we go. Now we'll see what they and their guarantee are made of. We know they won't burn millions of dollars on this."

Michelle grasped the immediate problem—the millions it would cost. And yet she knew the change she was ushering in was critical to business success.

So she modeled customer championship—the change— by going onto the message board the next day and telling everyone who had booked the $1 fare to Fiji to "Have a good trip" (in English and Fijian, no less). Travelocity would honor the fare, a first in the industry.

Every employee—on the edge of their seats for a day between the first news stories and Michelle's post—learned about this move. Here was the CEO modeling the behavior of the change she was leading. She had a board, Wall Street, and a boss at her parent company to answer to, but she still did it.

I'm told you could hear a pin drop at the call centers. As Michelle recalls now, had she instead rationalized a different decision, she likely would never have recovered internally, and the guarantee would likely never have been launched, or it would have fizzled out quickly.

Instead, some fifteen years later, the guarantee remains Travelocity's differentiator in the marketplace. Travelocity's tagline now is "Wander wisely," in part a nod to its "Customer first" guarantee, which is front and center among Travelocity's offerings and is even more generous today than when it launched.

This is how someone who believes in the change she's calling for puts everything on the line to model the change and get people to overcome their cognitive dissonance and realize the change is real. Michelle was determined that this terrible event wouldn't stifle the guarantee. In the end, it actually ensured the success of the guarantee, with call center agents—now convinced this was real change—making it possible.

"Changing process and culture is always hard," Michelle says now. "Creating deep-rooted belief has to be earned. It's a show-me world. And so sometimes, the biggest challenges, turned on their head, can create the greatest momentum for change." (For more on this story, see References.)

CONSISTENCY MATTERS

We don't often get such clear opportunities to model change. But we do often get opportunities to do things that are inconsistent with a change—to rationalize away any solution that would be easier than doing something hard that's aligned with the change.

And our people are watching. They don't want to change. They're like us—suffering from cognitive dissonance when we learn that we must do more than order the change...that we must model the change if we can have any hope we'll be successful with the change we want.

FIGHTING COGNITIVE DISSONANCE

So how do we overcome cognitive dissonance?

STEP ONE: FOCUS ON OURSELVES

The first step in any twelve-step program is to recognize our own problems! We have to be aware that we're likely to have ideas that run through our minds—even values that we hold—that are counter to others' realities. ("You mean I have to change, too?" "What do you mean you don't believe us about the guarantee?") And we have to be ready for them, take them in, and deal with them.

One way to do it is to simply get out there. Seek out and listen to a speech by someone you disagree with and let the brain process this different point of view without judgment. Notice how you feel during this experience. Change the TV to an uncomfortable channel and stay there for a while. Attend a church different from yours—or if you aren't a practitioner or believer, go to a place of worship—and listen without discounting what's being said. Books about other people's journeys can also be helpful in getting us out of a rut. While I was writing this, my daughters were reading *The Diary of a Young Girl* by Anne Frank and *To Kill A Mockingbird* by Harper Lee; both very much got me out of my rut as I participated in reading them.

Tony Hsieh, the CEO of uber-successful Zappos, is a good example of someone who gets out of his normal on a regular basis. "I try to do one uncomfortable thing every day," he says. It's indeed uncomfortable to get out of our normal, but it will exercise our processing muscles.

In my own professional and personal life, I've learned of a stress-management practice that helps me separate myself from my own thoughts and observe my thinking from outside myself. I learned it during a course developed by the Cleveland Clinic and offered at GE. Labeled "stress management," it was actually about *mindfulness*. It's not as new age or trendy as you might think.

With mindfulness, I find myself able to change my moods more easily. When I'm in a nonpreferred mood, I'll wake up to the fact that I'm in such a mood, step away, and ask myself, "What got me into this mood in the first place?" I'll often realize something minor is affecting me unnecessarily. If it's something bigger—something that will continue to affect me, like a change I need to make—I'm able to confront it much more easily by identifying it, openly thinking about it, and digesting it a bit more. This can help my immediate mood and allow my subconscious to take over as I digest whatever big item I'm dealing with.

Once we've learned to recognize and overcome our own cognitive dissonance, it's possible to help other people see the behaviors they will want to change.

STEP TWO: RECOGNIZE OTHERS' COGNITIVE DISSONANCE

Second, we recognize that our people and our peers are facing cognitive dissonance, and we need to help them with the personal behaviors they have to change.

We can't do this only logically because deep-rooted change in behavior (the kind that endures) stems from communicating both logically and emotionally with people. So how can we reach people emotionally? Well, we can model the change ourselves—and we can share with people that we, too, are struggling with the change. We open ourselves up when we do this, it makes the change more real, it opens up a conversation *with* our team and peers, not just *to* them, and it builds trust. We can even listen, asking our people for their ideas for solving the problem at the root of the change; people want to be heard, and they'll do extraordinary things when they feel heard, as we'll discuss later in the book.

Also, once our change effort has had some successes—even if small—we can celebrate these successes and communicate about them. When people see success, it makes the change real and less scary. It builds momentum. This gets our people to a new reality, a place where they're now more likely to loosen their resistance and consider the change at hand. As long as they recognize the change is a long journey—not finished once we've had a little success—they'll see this progress as positive, and it can break down the dissonance they started with.

ONWARD

Now that we're aware of our own cognitive dissonance, we

can see things more clearly. We can even get our heads around the fact that outdated ideas we hold won't serve us well. We'll learn more about that in Chapter 3.

CHAPTER TWO

- Cognitive dissonance is an enemy of change.
- Cognitive dissonance is the psychological discomfort we get when a value or deeply held belief of ours comes into question.
- In life, we all try to avoid cognitive dissonance by avoiding discussions about things we might disagree on.
- In business, as leaders, the more success we have, the stronger the belief that our way of doing things is *the* normal.
- We experience cognitive dissonance when we learn we have to get our hands dirty and get personally involved in a change effort.
- Our people experience cognitive dissonance when they find out that the way we've always done this is not the way we'll do it anymore.
- To succeed with change, we have to become aware of our own cognitive dissonance and also be thoughtful and mindful of our people's cognitive dissonance—what they're going through. We have to give them someone to follow.

Enemy #2

Our Outdated Ideas About Communications

A former colleague—someone about a dozen years older than me—once described his early career days as an operations analyst at a US automaker in the 1970s. Among other things, he told me how this company color-coded the memos it sent to white-collar employees. Memos (physical pieces of paper back then) were put in your inbox (a physical item on your desk that your assistant would fill with new mail when she [usually it was a she in those days] also cleared out your outbox stacked just below your inbox). This was pretty straightforward.

But when you got a blue memo, it was from a senior executive. Everyone stopped what they were doing to read the blue memos. People went to each other's offices and talked about what the memo said, what the marching orders were, and what it would mean.

"You looked at your blue letters before anything else," he told me. "They were gospel."

In those days, communications was still a pretty straightforward thing. Employees had little or no information outside what was in the memos, so they largely accepted what they read.

THINGS HAVE CHANGED

Outdated beliefs about the magic of communications—the written documents, emails, videos, town halls, staff meetings, intranet articles, stories, planning sessions, pamphlets, tweets, visual treatments, etc.—are another enemy of change, especially change programs. The fact is these kinds of communications are absolutely necessary, but they're not a silver bullet.

Traditional communication—and lots of it—is critical to any change program. Stories with examples of the change at your organization can be particularly potent; they can inspire or, at least, help people envision or grasp where you're headed. In fact, storytelling—talking about successes during the change—can make the change less scary or foreign and more relatable. (I believe storytelling is so powerful that I've included three dozen stories in this book.)

The volume of traditional communications is also key. Insigniam, one of the most successful change management consultancies I've witnessed in action, says, "Your message must be so prevalent that it's dripping from the walls of your organization."

It's true that we must explain the challenge the organization is facing if it doesn't change. We need to tell everyone where we're headed, tell them again, and tell them again. When we're communicating three times more than we think we should, we may (*may*) be reaching people; some experts have seen organizations communicate only 10 percent as much as they should.

We think we're overcommunicating, but our people likely aren't hearing it. One CEO was caught bragging to his consultants about how heavily involved he was in the change; the consultants then spoke to line managers, who told them they had hardly heard from the CEO about the change. Surprise!

This is all too common. I've often heard managers say, "But we sent an email that was very clear." Do you remember a song the very first time you hear it? Usually not. Only with repetition do we even become aware of most songs. Only after hearing it many times do we actually learn a song. And those are songs we *want* to hear and learn; news about change often comes in unwanted.

All the Communications in the World...

Intranet Articles   Emails   Newsletters   Videos   Town Halls   Staff Meetings   Pamphlets   Social Media Posts   TV Reports   Focus Groups   One-on-Ones   Blogs   Posters   Visual Treatments   Handouts   Flyers on Seats   White Papers   News Articles   Rinse Wash Repeat   Intranet Articles   Emails   Newsletters   Videos   Town Halls   Staff Meetings   Pamphlets   Social Media Posts   TV Reports   Focus Groups One-on-Ones   Blogs   Posters   Visual Treatments   Handouts   Flyers on Seats   White Papers   News Articles   Rinse Wash Repeat

Of course, we're guaranteed to get bored and to tell ourselves that we sound like a broken record. That's because we're hearing ourselves talk every time; no one else is hearing us anywhere close to every time.

Take heart, though. Imagine how bored the people at GEICO must be. How many times have they said that thing about "fifteen minutes"? How many different ways have they laid it up for us (cavemen, a gecko, a camel, and so on)? GEICO's advertising is proof positive that message repetition works.

I was once part of a leadership team so tired of communicating the same messages over and over that—for a town hall—we held our own version of Saturday Night Live and found all kinds of creative ways to insert the messages. The Church Lady told anyone who couldn't recite our values to "Scoot, scoot, you sinner!"

All the Communications in the World... Won't Matter If Our Actions Aren't Aligned

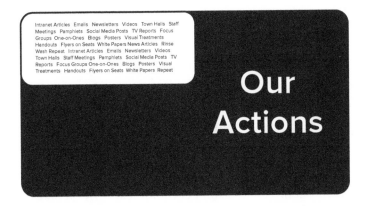

Intranet Articles Emails Newsletters Videos Town Halls Staff Meetings Pamphlets Social Media Posts TV Reports Focus Groups One-on-Ones Blogs Posters Visual Treatments Handouts Flyers on Seats White Papers News Articles Rinse Wash Repeat Intranet Articles Emails Newsletters Videos Town Halls Staff Meetings Pamphlets Social Media Posts TV Reports Focus Groups One-on-Ones Blogs Posters Visual Treatments Handouts Flyers on Seats White Papers Repeat

Our Actions

Hard as it can be, this repetitive communication keeps the change on track. It informs people of what the change is, it helps them grasp how they might engage, it lets them know about progress, and it helps build momentum. And—as we'll see later in the book—if it's done incongruently, with some leaders saying one thing and others saying something different, it can be deadly.

POOF...IT'S NOT MAGIC

But if we think this is all we need, we're fooling ourselves. Traditional communications work—alone—doesn't overcome the natural resistance that exists in each of those people going through the process. All these rational communications, the blue memos saying, "We *are* going to do this," "You guys will need to do things differently," and "Look at how our competitor is eating our lunch," won't make sustained believers out of those who are having change thrust upon them. It—alone—won't make them *want* to change.

And it simply won't overcome actions by anyone above them that are inconsistent with the changes they're being told or asked to forge. Remember, our people are dying to see inconsistent actions. They're dying to hear and compare inconsistent communications. Inconsistent actions and communications are their lifeline giving them hope—consciously or subconsciously—that the change isn't necessary or won't happen. All the logical written and spoken communications in the world can be killed by inconsistent action.

ACTIONS VS. WORDS

Early in my career, I had to learn the power of actions versus words and learn it the hard way.

This was when I led labor communications as a consultant and later in-house. I wrote a lot of communications to various work groups about negotiations, I spoke to media about this, and I helped managers think through what we would communicate, how, when, and to whom. It was basic communications—written word, spoken word, broadcast word: what we think of when we normally think of the word "communications."

The company I was helping was going through some tough times financially. It had, for some time, communicated its direction through "plans," and it announced it was transitioning away from its great growth plan, but it didn't announce what it was transitioning to. This brought about a lot of consternation and confusion among employees, especially one work group that was negotiating with this company. After some pretty gnarly and public negotiations, these employees walked off the job. In striking, they said they felt management simply didn't respect them.

Management was certain that the union would crumble, that it couldn't organize itself well enough to pull off a successful strike, especially given how previous negotiations had been so one-sided in management's favor. But these workers held together, and the company was brought to its knees.

In the aftermath of the strike, one senior executive at this business was interviewed, and he said something like, "We just didn't communicate well enough to these employees."

As the person on the ground creating the communications, I was discouraged by this.

I remember asking a client of mine—someone at the company who was a mentor—about what this executive had said. "Did we miss something?" I asked. "Clearly given that they struck, the communications could have been better, but how?" I wanted to learn.

"Al," this mentor said, "we communicated and communicated and communicated to these employees, but it wasn't the kind of communications you're thinking of. When we negotiated with them for the last contract and extracted work rule changes that we didn't ask for from other groups, we were communicating to them—telling them we didn't respect them. When we brought them in for training last summer to show them videos of customers complaining about their work, we were communicating to them, and it was much more than what was in that training; our action—making it such a big deal—was communication in itself. When we told them they wouldn't be fired if they struck, but they could be 'permanently replaced,' we were communicating to them; 'fired' and 'permanent replacement' sound enough alike that they had to figure we thought they were just dumb.

"We didn't respect these people, Al, and we told them this over and over again. I was just as guilty as anyone else in all of this, now that I've had time to reflect on it. What people don't understand, and what you need to understand if you're ever going to make a difference as a communications person, is that we're foolish if we convince ourselves that written communications and videos shipped to houses, that sort of thing, is some sort of magic potion. Our communications is not what we write about; it's what we do."

My young self was taken aback by this. To think that all of my product, resulting from a lot of hard work, meant only a small part of what we communicated—well, this was humbling and illuminating for me.

I'm glad I learned this early in my career. As a result, the way I thought about and practiced communications changed significantly.

IT'S IN WHAT WE DO

So it's in our actions. We see this in a McKinsey & Company's survey of the one-third of organizations that were successful with their change initiatives. They listed action-oriented communications tactics as three of their four most successful moves for mobilizing people: "celebrating successes, symbolic actions," "clear executive sponsorship," and "mobilizing...change leaders to model desired changes."

We also see this in the communications field. Today, the

Arthur W. Page Society, the leading organization of top corporate communicators in the world, has made this concept—the power of action as communications—one of its Page Principles. "Prove it with action," they say. "Public perception of an enterprise is determined 90 percent by what it does and 10 percent by what it says." (Full disclosure, I'm a member of the organization.)

This might seem ironic. These leaders grew up as professionals and rose to the top of their fields by being good at writing. This was their life's work. They had honed their skills. It was what they and their teams were known for in their organizations. And yet they say all this kind of work is only 10 percent of the communications equation for an organization.

Clearly, they've had experiences like mine where they learned we can't communicate our way out of a problem if the action doesn't match. These leaders in the field may have started in the days of color-coded memos, but those days are over.

Today's modern communications leaders bring much greater value when advising executives and clients about being true to their word, lest the organization lose all credibility. Written communication is still the must-punch ticket to succeed in the communications field, but it's by no means the most crucial value that leading communicators bring.

It can't be. Why? Because of technology.

Today our employees are no longer captive to blue memos from senior executives. With the rise of ubiquitous information available twenty-four hours a day, employees can see what we're telling our investors, customers, the media, and other stakeholders—even what we're saying to other employee groups.

From this, they can piece together even more clearly what we're actually doing. And they can easily compare all of what we're saying and doing out there to what we're saying to them. They even can comment on—and call out—the differences.

Some employees are going to be on board no matter what. Some will spend all of their time trying to find the inconsistencies. They'll go on Glassdoor or some other app and expose us to everyone else. The large majority are open to being swayed—by us, and by the skeptics inside the walls. We can't get rid of all the skeptics or what they say, but we make change easier on everyone by acting consistently with what we say.

This whole way of thinking—that we live in a new world with ubiquitous information where old-world communications tactics don't have the same capacity—was the genesis for the Arthur W. Page Society's seminal work:

The Authentic Enterprise. It's a great work even if it's more than a decade old. It's changed the trajectory of a major field that influences corporations and society, and I highly recommend a read of it. (It's brief.) But if I have to sum it up in a few words, I'd be a bit less erudite than the original and say, "If you think you can fool people by saying one thing and doing another, stop that. Your stakeholders (including your people) are smarter and more informed than you think. Be authentic."

When it comes to communicating change initiatives, it's just as much about authentically showing people the change through action.

SHOWING THE WAY

Take the leader of a top office furniture manufacturer head-quartered in the Midwest. As a design thinker, he had been in the business of transforming other businesses—through their office spaces—his whole career. But when he was attempting to transform his own business, it wasn't going as smoothly.

The company, which builds and re-creates workspaces for new and emerging ways to work, is headquartered in historically hardworking Dutch country in Western Michigan, along with some of its competitors. The corporate headquarters had just installed collaboration spaces—open areas with couches and comfy chairs where people can collaborate and brainstorm.

In doing so, the company used its own people's work—their modern design point of view, technologies, and products, as well as the organization's values on sustainability—the very things it was marketing worldwide. They had already overhauled to like-new an old manufacturing building into a headquarters, giving it flexible capabilities so it could be transformed regularly and cost-effectively into whatever was needed by the next business iteration.

The next business iteration was now collaboration spaces, and that's what the organization reused some space for. For the company's leader, it was critical that his people learn this new way of working. This wasn't just a matter of using the business's product—it was a matter of staying competitive in a world that's ever-changing. He'd seen the success that social spaces brought to other parts of his global business, and he'd seen how his customers' employees were changing as a result of this kind of space. He wanted the same result for his own headquarters.

So the building now included these open, clean-lined spaces. They looked cool, and the leader was excited that his team members now had access to them. The problem was that very few people who worked there were using these social areas. They were almost empty. Ironically, this company that was ushering these spaces into office buildings in 150 countries around the world wasn't spending much time in its own social space. Was it a change too far?

This leader asked someone on his team why no one was using the space.

The colleague said something like, "You know, you've built a great midwestern company with a really strong work ethic. People believe in being heads-down in their cubicles. If they go anywhere other than the bathroom or the cafeteria, it's to a conference room for a meeting. They'd get a funny look from people if they sat on those comfy sofas we put out there."

So here he was. Not only was he trying to bring his own organization's thinking into his business headquarters, but he was also, in a way, trying to transform his business. He recognized that his business was grounded in a great past, but he didn't want it to miss the future. What to do?

He started modeling the behavior he wanted to see. He upended his calendar and held all of his one-on-one meetings in the collaboration area instead of his office. And he convinced his direct reports to do the same. He set a precedent, and nowadays it's often hard to find a spot in the collaboration space.

It was the beginning of a long path to get people to really

change beyond going to this space for more than coffee. It was the beginning of reshaping the culture. But it started with the leader modeling the behavior. It started with him communicating through action—because communication through words (newsletters saying that people need to learn how to collaborate in new ways) well, that wasn't going to cut it.

AGELESS AND NEW

This success through action is a great example of how the ratio between what we say and what we do is the real factor in communications. And this idea is actually ageless.

Arthur W. Page, who led AT&T's communications for more than twenty years, said it well—even if in 1950s parlance—in a speech to other executives: "A company's reputation is chiefly dependent upon what it does and in a lesser degree on what it says and this lesser degree becomes very small indeed if what it says and what it does do not jibe."

Ralph Waldo Emerson, John F. Kennedy, Benjamin Franklin and many others have had similar takes on this topic. As Franklin said, "Words may show a man's wit, but actions his meaning."

To put a finer point on this, I'll share what a former colleague I worked with some time ago warned when speaking to a management meeting: "Your people watch you go to the bathroom."

He paused pregnantly, his audience perplexed and looking around the room with a nervous chuckle. Clearly everyone was wondering where this was going.

"I'm not saying that they watch you *in* the bathroom," he said. "No. They watch you *go to* the bathroom. They've got eyes on you every minute you're working and every time you leave your desk. You come back from a meeting with your head down, and they worry. You make the slightest joke about an initiative, and you can sink it. You don't show up for a meeting about something without explaining why you missed it and without expressing support for the initiative being discussed, and the initiative could get set back. Everything's riding on you. Don't forget that."

Let's take that executive's advice. His point is that leaders at all levels are powerful people, whether we like it or want it. Even when we wish we aren't being watched, we're being watched, and our actions are communicating things. And let's add to it that we've asked our people to change, that change is hard, that it causes resistance, forcing our people to want to go back to the fetal position. And let's recognize that our every action can make or break the change.

Not only must we overcome our own discomfort—whether

tied to the change itself or to the belief that we don't need to get our hands fully dirty and model the change—but we also must help our people overcome theirs.

This is where communicating by showing them the way—rather than simply telling them the way—makes change more real, more comfortable (or less uncomfortable), more necessary, more believable, and more palatable. The very people who will make or break the change need us to show them the way; that makes us every bit a part of the group driving that change.

The good news is we can accept this new (and ageless) communications reality that our behavioral changes will be central to successful change. The bad news is it's hard. It's hard for leaders to accept we'll have to change, and it's harder still to actually do the changing. It's especially hard for people who've gotten to where we are because we're naturally one way or because we've learned and ingrained in ourselves the way to be—which is now being changed.

Given how uncomfortable this news can be for leaders, I can't fault change management consultants for not coming out and saying it as boldly as our example at the beginning of the book did. But I'm here to point out our shortcomings in the area of change so we can all learn to change—not only so we can avoid these weaknesses but also so we can learn how to be better leaders every day and during change.

HOW DO WE CHANGE?

So how do we get our heads around the change so we can be more comfortable when our people are observing us, when they're trying to decide whether this change is real? It helps if those above us are modeling the change for us so we have something to follow, but let's say that's not the case, or let's say there's no one above us.

The first step is to believe in the change. As we'll discuss later, it's best if each of us has had a say in the change process early, so we're somewhat bought-in, no matter where we sit in the organization. Either way, it's our responsibility as leaders to find a way to believe in the change. This can be hard, especially if we aren't excited about the change—whether we have cognitive dissonance, or we simply don't agree with it. (And if we really can't buy in to the change, we have a different set of choices to make.) We simply have to get to a place where we believe in it. As we'll discuss later, one leader calls the idea of committing to a change when we don't agree with it "have a backbone: disagree and commit."

Once we believe in it (or commit to it) from inside ourselves, our mindset shifts. This isn't an overnight thing; it's something we must deliberately work on. We must consciously find the rational things about the change that we agree with (or at least understand) and psych ourselves up to authentically support them. This can be hard, but it's necessary.

The second step is to deliberately act out the modeling. Think about our day-to-day work, the language we use regularly, the emphasis made clear by our calendars. Is any of it inconsistent with the change? How can we make it more congruent with the change? Are there some obvious ways we can change these things to align with it more clearly? Are there some ways to communicate—by our actions—that this is for real?

This has to be deliberate work that we each undertake for the change to be successful among those who we lead. We can't rationalize away things in our day-to-day work or our behavior if they're inconsistent with the change. And we have to be honest with ourselves—and even, at times, with our own people, who need to see our struggles so they feel less lonely during the change—if we struggle and catch ourselves going off-change somehow. (There is more on modeling in Chapter 11.)

LEARNING MORE

Finally, if you weren't in tune with the latest thinking in the communications space, I hope this chapter brought you closer to it. Even though we know intellectually that this thinking is true, it's easy to forget this in our day-to-day struggle to make change happen. Here are a few other ways we can defeat this enemy of change.

First, expect your communications leader to demand this

behavior of you. If you're a senior leader, you may approach your communications leader and say, "We need to change our organization, and we need to do it by painting a great picture of the future, a future where we move away from command and control to unleash the creative juices of our workforce. Your communications will be a critical part of this effort."

When you say all of this to them, when you say their communications work will be critical, your communicator should say something back to you, like, "So will yours, boss." (Professionally, of course!)

If you're any part of a change effort at any level in the organization, bring your communications team into the change and get their ideas and support for how you can use action to further the change you're trying to make. They should be ready to help because today's communications professionals have a greater stake than ever in what the organization says *and* in what it does. Getting the organization's "say:do" ratio to 100 percent is their North Star. And when you tell them you think communications will be central to your change management program, don't be surprised—don't have cognitive dissonance—when they tell you communications has a lot to do with what *you* do. They're just trying to help us all overcome an enemy of change; they're trying to defeat any outdated ideas about communications.

Second, as mentioned above, be willing to *tell your people how hard the change is for you* (provided this is true). Be willing to communicate your missteps that were counter to the change. Admitting to imperfection and sharing the work we're doing on ourselves—this leads our people in the right direction; it tells them that they're not alone, that their missteps are OK, too, so they can keep going, keep pushing, keep wanting to change.

Third, it may help you to stay abreast of what's going on in the communications field, especially at its leading edge. They aren't debating punctuation; they're focused on integration, trust, corporate character, and so much more. One way to do this is to read *The Authentic Enterprise*, as well as *The New Era of the CCO* and other more recent work from the Arthur W. Page Society, at Page.org.

IN SUM

What's the bottom line? If our change management efforts are going to work, we need to use modern communications thinking, not staid ideas about traditional communications as a magic potion. Ironically, modern communications thinking uses the ageless principle that authenticity and action communicate much more clearly and effectively than words alone ever will.

CHAPTER THREE

- Outdated ideas about communications are an enemy of change.
- To be sure, we need lots of traditional communications—emails, town halls, focus groups, you name it—and these communications should be "dripping from the walls."
- But traditional communications is only 10 percent of the equation. Today, with the advent of new media, people have many more ways to get their information than fifty years ago.
- Communications is 90 percent action and 10 percent words.
- Our people—with their cognitive dissonance and their access to all kinds of information—are naturally looking for inconsistencies in our "say:do" ratio because these are potential signs that the change isn't serious.
- So what we say and what we do must be aligned—always—but especially during change.
- The best way to show we're serious is to communicate by modeling the change.

BUT GANDHI NEVER ACTUALLY SAID THAT

While writing this book, I explained to numerous people that leaders need to model the change they want to see in their organizations. Many of them told me, "Oh, it's like what Gandhi said: 'You must be the change you wish to see in the world.'"

Exactly. I told them I intended to include Gandhi somewhere in the book. This was true, of course. So you may be wondering why I haven't used the quote (and won't use it).

When trying to find specific evidence of the quote, I started online, but I couldn't find proper source material. I dusted off my ancient physical copy of *Bartlett's Familiar Quotations*, and it's not among Gandhi's listed quotes.

Stumped, I searched further. Turns out, there is no written evidence Gandhi ever actually said this. According to Quote Investigator, the closest Gandhi ever came to saying this was when he said the following:

"If we could change ourselves, the tendencies in the world would also change. As a man changes his own nature, so does the attitude of the world change towards him...We need not wait to see what others do."

So where did this "be the change" quote originate? In my searches, I've seen quote experts attribute it to both bumper sticker writers and coffee mug designers, as well as someone named Arleen Lorrance for a work of hers called the Love Project in 1974—twenty-six years after Gandhi's death. Even Lorrance's quote isn't a match to what we see on coffee mugs.

I really wish Gandhi had said it...it would have made my job much easier if I could have just pointed to that guy.

FOUR

Enemy #3

We Let Inertia Get in the Way

The scene is the same conference room where the change management guru (the "jerk") pitched her services at the beginning of the book. But this is a flashback. The executive team is just starting to grapple with the problem at hand.

Sitting around a nicely stained table, with walls of high-end paneling, with views of blue skies and nothing else because we're at the top of the building, the top executives at this firm are engaged in a deep conversation, with the CFO finishing a presentation.

CFO: So those are the numbers. We've fallen from first to third in the past year in sales volume and profit margin. It's not pretty, Jim.

CEO: Thanks, Tom. I have to say, I'm tired of losing. I mean, we have a strong balance sheet and good margins, but we keep falling behind Nexition and Astorcast. I've met their CEOs and some of their executives, and I don't get it. They aren't any smarter than we are. We know more about this business than they do. We have a better product pipeline than them. But they keep moving faster than us. I'm scratching my head. I want to open up to you guys: I'm losing sleep at night. I'm not sure what to do anymore. So I'm hoping we can openly talk about what we need to do to be competitive again. Nothing's off the table. You're free to give me all your ideas.

Various people respond to the CEO. The communications leader says she's hearing from many managers that morale is low. The HR leader says it's actually starting to hurt recruiting. The conversation continues.

CFO: I just wonder what we need to do differently...what we need to change. I know change programs are hard, but it seems like we need to do something radical if we're going to change our trajectory.

CEO: You know, what I'm hearing is that this isn't a one-off problem. The trajectory of our future is going to be determined by how we address this. What can we do?

The mood in the room becomes open and collaborative.

People open up about their fears and offer ideas for the challenge at hand. There's a contagion growing around the table. The group starts talking about what their organization needs to do differently to change things. There's a recognition of underinvestment in IT; this is slowing supply chain and operations, and this hurts delivery time to customers.

COO: I think there's real merit in what I'm hearing. We're going to have to change as an organization. Doing what we're talking about—investing in IT—is going to require cutbacks in other areas, hard cutbacks I'm sure. But how do we do tha—

Then, out of the blue, the building's fire alarm goes off. The executives have to go out to the parking lot like everyone else. And it's a perfect time for people to hit them up and talk shop. They're approached by people who need to talk to them. Hot topics, long-term topics, "That analysis you asked me to do for you"...all sorts of colleagues approach them in the course of the twenty minutes when everyone is stuck in the parking lot.

The fire drill ends, and the executives go back to their calendars, with meetings the rest of the day. Two weeks pass, and at the next meeting of this group, the Sales Leader and CFO bring heartening news. They've won some big orders. And the numbers finally look a little better, with two regions outperforming the competition.

Communications Leader: So do we want to get back to our conversation from a couple weeks ago, about the change?

CEO: I think it's a good idea. I think it makes sense for us to put a subteam on the subject and explore it some more. I'm going to ask the two of you to put that together. (*Pointing to the COO and communications leader.*) Now let's get back to the business at hand.

For the COO and Communications Leader, there's excitement at first, but it peters out. Eventually, with waning support, the great idea has died. It was good at the time. It was wonderful that the team recognized at some level that the organization needed to change. But clearly this is—at best—a baby-steps effort.

COMMONPLACE

You think this could never happen? Well, I've personally witnessed something like this multiple times. (Peers of mine have as well.)

As groups and individuals, we all have lightbulb moments, times when an idea takes over in our head or in a conversation with others. People love getting outside the everyday and having a think. Unfortunately, we don't always follow through on our genius thoughts. The team here had a breakthrough and realized it would have to do something hard. But with time, inertia set in.

Inertia is another enemy of change.

While the word "inertia" has its place in the lexicon of physics and other sciences (meaning lack of movement), and while it can be synonymous with "laziness" and even "sloth," I'm not claiming that we've entered the scientific realm or become lazy. We work hard, but sometimes, important things don't move forward in any case. When we allow inertia to get in the way, it can hurt—it can even kill—what is much-needed change, putting us further behind the eight ball. It happens for a number of reasons.

OTHER STUFF GETS IN THE WAY

The fire alarm in the scene above instantly transported the executives around that table from a moment of clarity back to everyday stuff. It's never bad to get unstructured time with employees, like a fire drill, but it took them away from the challenge at hand: the deep thinking that was needed to build sustained consensus around an idea as hard as the need for significant change. And once the drill was over, they went back to their deadlines, customer demands, "gotta minutes?" and opinions being sought. This takes a significant amount of energy and cognition for the executive. Brain activity increases. Stress levels rise thanks to increased adrenaline and cortisol being pumped through the body.

This stress-inducing other stuff is often what many executives thrive on. Human history includes tens of thousands of years in straight survival mode; those who survived—those who were the very best at living in constant stress—passed along their genes to us. With all this hormone production designed to support fight or flight, the body and brain aren't in any shape to continue the clarity around a big idea.

Even executive retreats run this hazard; I've been a part of teams that have decided at our off-sites to take on some initiative or other, only to have it lose steam once back at the office, once "today" issues came up.

A division leader I worked for at one company used to talk about a mythical thing; he called it "time to think." He had a desire to schedule into his day or his week or his month some "away time." But it remained a dreamed-of thing, not something that I ever heard him say he had actually done.

In my experience, large organizations like his seem to add complexity to their own complexity, adding activities that make the load unnecessarily heavy for executives, thus, making it almost impossible to have time to reflect.

If an executive at a multibillion-dollar business unit isn't flying around the world to see customers, she's off to regional affinity group meetings that she sponsors, she's taking a three-day trip to China to support a peer's joint venture, or she's spending a week away at the company's training academy as an "executive in residence," where she teaches or speaks to classes, meets with high-potential employees and grabs beers at night to network with younger people who are looking for exposure to key executives.

It's "now, now, now" for these executives. As a young employee, I used to think leaders like this must have been superhuman, given how little sleep they got. But—having been put in such situations in my own career and worked with many peers who have—I've come to realize that all this activity can cause inertia around big-picture thinking, the soul-searching that could lead to fresh thinking. No human—even those who we believe might be superhuman somehow—can take as much cognition and also drive the kind of change needed. There's simply too much other stuff.

If we're going to overcome this "other stuff" conundrum, we simply must make time away from the here and now— for ourselves to think and for our teams. As we'll talk about later in this chapter, we have to rid ourselves of some tactical work to get the needed time to think. Plus, we must have time to support our efforts and build momentum, which we'll talk about next.

LACK OF SUPPORT, MOMENTUM

I was working on a new initiative at GE that I started about eighteen months after joining. At that point, despite a rather hectic bout of sink-or-swim-itis, I still had questions about how stuff got done in that company—how big initiatives, like turning an eighty-year-old, $20 billion business unit into one that could take full advantage of digital capabilities and thinking...how these kinds of efforts succeeded or failed. I was talking with a colleague and telling him I was unsure what might stop my efforts; I asked him about this so I might avoid whatever pitfall I might not realize was right ahead of me.

He said, "You know, in my fifteen years here, I've never seen an initiative get stopped. People don't stop initiatives. Things just die for lack of support."

Change initiatives can't build momentum without support, and they require a sense of urgency. To get momentum and urgency, they need buy-in from frontline employees—the very people who will have to change their own way of thinking and of doing things. These people need to see the change modeled. If it's a sense of urgency we want to drive, we have to show them a sense of urgency. If it's a particular change in how we work, we have to work that way first.

Without an example to follow, stemming from leadership that buys in to the change being called for, middle managers have a much harder time standing before their people and modeling the change themselves, so they can't support the change adequately enough to convince employees that the change is real.

No support, no momentum.

NEW DATA

New data—like the improved near-term performance announced by the CFO and sales leader two weeks later in the scenario at the beginning of the chapter—can bring about inertia. At publicly traded companies, the here and now often eats the future, and the latest data can drown out the need for long-term change. We can either relax (we shouldn't relax, but sometimes we do) if the news is good, or we have to quickly figure out what this news means if the news is bad.

New data can also bring about inertia-inducing doubts about whether the change we've chosen is the right change. "Well, we decided to go in this direction, but now we see our competitor going in that direction. Maybe we need to slow down for a while to see how their change works out."

This sort of thing can happen, especially in organizations that have short attention spans, in places where the buy-in about the change isn't deep among leaders, or where the change isn't deliberately designed around our own organization's future, based on our own deep market insights and our deeply held beliefs—our values—for our own organization.

As we'll see later, we need to focus on *our* true north—based on the problem we've all reached consensus on, and on unimpeachable principles—and not let extraneous information get in our way.

LACK OF CLARITY OR ALIGNMENT

Another cause of inertia: lack of clarity around what exactly we're going for and why. This can result when some leaders simply aren't aligned with the change. Certainly, building consensus around the need for change—the why—and a vision for the new future, including a specific set of goals, can take a lot of time, energy, and thinking. This often involves seeking and taking input from dozens or hundreds of employees—or even the whole organization.

The leadership team starts its thinking using these ideas and must determine what a renewed future looks like, what success will be, and other measurable and paintable factors. It must build alignment among leaders for all of this. And while there needs to be room for different paths to the organization's true north—given that so many things can change during a change process—people need clear direction and an exciting future. Without clarity and a "steady as it goes" mentality—even through a naturally uneasy change process—the effort can be exhausting for our people.

Without all members of senior leadership aligned, able to easily speak about the challenge and to model the future in the same way, confusion can abound. Remember, employees don't naturally want to change; if they detect uncertainty or a lack of clarity about what the change is, they can be as confused as they choose.

Lack of clarity is one more excuse they have to not change. We'll talk later in the book about how to get clarity and how to communicate in harmony.

DIGESTION

When leaders come to terms with all that's involved in a change—how much is prescribed for us, just how different certain things will look—it takes time to digest it all. This "getting our heads around it" process can cause inertia.

Just as it takes frontline employees and middle managers time to come to terms with how their work lives will have to change, it can also take executives time to understand the change and communicate the change properly.

"Wait. Time out," I've heard executives say. "If we're going to do this thing we've always done but do it to match the change we're going for, how should we do it going forward? Do we need to change anything? Or is this process in synch with the change?"

Everyone deserves time to digest, but if it's allowed to run amok, it can cause change-damaging or even change-killing inertia.

FATIGUE

Because change is now a constant in our organizations, we're very likely to confront change fatigue throughout the organization. Even though *our* change effort is the most important our organization has faced, our people may lack the energy to drive it. According to a recent targeted study by Gagen MacDonald, a firm focused on driving the cultural (or heart) aspects of change, navigating change fatigue is the single biggest challenge for those trying to drive it.

Gagen MacDonald makes the argument that the enemy of fatigue is energy. What drives passion and energy? Certainly, the absence of support from leadership won't bring energy. Instead, passion from leaders—where leaders show employees the way, where they communicate and celebrate successes and milestones with the team along the way—plus engagement of the team during the planning process—can make a huge difference in attitudes. It's about getting our people to *want* to change. (We'll learn more about engaging our people in the change in Chapter 10.)

Another kind of fatigue: energy slumps. After a year to eighteen months, it's very easy for people to tire out during a transformation. (I know. We thought we'd be done in eighteen months. Not so fast. These efforts can take years if they're going to really endure.) We've had so much change and so much talk of change; plus, our people are still holding down their day jobs. So it's only natural that progress can slow, allowing inertia to build.

Bain & Company focuses a lot of its change management work on this factor, and they tell us that when this happens, it's an important time for the senior managers to—themselves—review the original goals, get excited about all the progress already made, and reenergize around the transformation going on. Without senior management's renewed vigor—visible for all to see—the exhaustion factor can seep deep into the organization. With senior managers digesting then showcasing successes and sharing a renewed excitement and optimism about the program, contagion can set in once again.

HOW DO WE FIGHT INERTIA?

I've listed some of the top causes of change-crippling inertia here. What's important is that we keep our eyes open, looking for signs that would signal that our change initiative is being dragged down by inertia of any kind.

We have to be deliberate about fighting inertia, and before we can ask others to do it, it has to start with each of us—as individuals—and how we manage our time. I have three suggestions to consider for overcoming personal inertia, and they all have to do with time management and prioritization. Then I have three suggestions regarding organizational inertia.

I've come to use a tool that was used by Dwight Eisenhower during World War II, and it may have been used earlier. I first learned about it from Stephen Covey's *The 7 Habits of Highly Effective People*. This is the "Urgent/Important Matrix." If you Google either "Eisenhower Urgent Important" or "Covey Urgent Important" and click on "Images," you'll find numerous iterations of it beyond the one I've developed myself here, which is the one I use. I've laminated it and keep it taped just below my computer screen in my office.

The basic idea is to look at things through the filter of how urgent something is and how important it is.

Urgent/Important Matrix

	Urgent	Not Urgent
Important	I • Crisis • Pressing problems • Firefighting • Major scrap and rework • Deadline-driven projects	II • Prevention • Production capability activities • Relationship building • Recognizing new opportunities • Planning • Re-creation
Not Important	III • Interruptions • Some calls • Some mail • Some reports • Some meetings • Proximate pressing matters • Popular activities • Some scrap and rework	IV • Trivia • Busywork • Some mail • Some phone calls • Time wasters • Pleasant activities

Source: Adapted in part from *The 7 Habits of Highly Effective People* (New York Free Press, 1989), 149-162.

Here's how I interpret this.

Quadrant I includes those things that are high in urgency and importance. These are things we often can't avoid, like crises, deadline-driven work...maybe even some change implementation. As young up-and-comers, we get to shine when we work in this quadrant, but the higher up we get, the more thoughtful we should be about how much of this work we take on (we must do some of it, to be sure) and how much we delegate. (Obviously, if something is change-related, we should be most careful about what we delegate versus do/model.)

Quadrant II includes things high in importance but low in urgency. Think relationship building, planning, developing people. We want to spend as much time as possible in this quadrant, and it becomes more essential the higher we go in an organization. In fact, the more we spend in quadrant II, the less we need to spend in quadrant I. Working on prevention can prevent crises later. Building relationships can make so many things run more smoothly. By developing people, we not only get fulfillment (I hope), but we also are training people to whom we can delegate things in quadrant I. Converting from quadrant I to quadrant II takes deliberate, intense effort (for example, we're doing the actual work plus teaching our delegates all at the same time), but reaching quadrant II allows the "time to think" that we discussed earlier in this chapter.

Quadrant III includes things that are urgent but not important. We've received three phone calls or emails from someone wanting to sell us something, so we return their inquiry. We go to that weekly meeting that isn't important to us, we rarely have anything to offer during the meeting, we get little information from it, and our absence won't be noticed. This can also include—if it's overdone—things like fantasy football, bracketology, the Oscar pool, etc., but fraternization is also relationship-building and re-creation—things in quadrant II. All work and no play really dulls all of us, but we just can't go overboard, or we won't be able to spend time on other crucial things in quadrant II.

Stay away from quadrant IV, the place with unimportant and nonurgent stuff. Think about how fulfilling it would be to spend time in quadrant II when you're tempted to spend time in quadrant IV.

MORE

The other suggestions come from books I've read, and they may help.

In *Deep Work: Rules for Focused Success in a Distracted World*, Cal Newport shares his principles for achieving complete focus when attacking difficult matters by getting completely free of distraction. While Newport is lucky that, as a professor, he can schedule his heavy classes in one semester so that in the next semester, he has a lighter load (and more time and cognitive capacity for deep work), I have actually practiced deep work with some success. No emails, no phone calls, just work. But I was only able to do so because a boss of mine read the book, gave it to all of us, and we blocked two hours a day—companywide—to conduct Deep Work. Although I had an office and could close my door, some people working in open spaces would simply turn the overhead lights off in their area to signify and remind anyone passing through that they were deep-working. Alas, the boss who introduced me to *Deep Work* didn't end up modeling this change (he scheduled meetings during deep work time), and others followed suit. But thanks for the book!

Then there's *Getting Things Done: The Art of Stress-Free Productivity* by David Allen. Allen suggests, among other practices, that you list every single thing on your to-do list—everything. He takes clients through their offices, computers and houses, documenting the work they have to do, from planting new flowers to visiting that new plant. According to Allen, once you've developed this exhaustive list, you have greater creative capacity because there aren't any unaccounted-for items to bother you or your subconscious. I know people who swear by this practice.

While we work on our own self-improvement—a lifelong effort, really—we need to also work together to fight organizational inertia, to create a sense of urgency organization-wide to overcome general complacency. John Kotter's *A Sense of Urgency* teaches us the importance of urgency and its enemy, complacency. Included is the idea that frenzied behavior can masquerade as urgency when it's just frenzied stuff that isn't moving the change forward. Look out for urgency killers like made-up crises. Act, live, and communicate every chance you get with a sense of urgency so everyone gets the idea from you.

We can also use the Urgent/Important Matrix throughout the enterprise to track whether we're tackling the change properly as a team. If all of us who are working on the change share the same frame of reference and use the same lingo, we can keep each other honest about whether we're only in crisis mode (quadrant I) or if we're making long-term progress so as to get out of crisis mode (quadrant II) and what we need to do differently to get from quadrant I to quadrant II.

Urgent/Important Matrix for the Enterprise

	Urgent	Not Urgent
Important	I • Fighting fires • Responding to critics • Responding to competitor moves • Immediate employee issues • Executive change	II • Planning and prevention • Employee engagement, growth • Customer relationships, research • Stakeholder relationships • Enterprise renewal (change)
Not Important	III • Constant strategy changes • Overreacting to competitors • Overreacting to news • Non-strategic "emergencies"	IV • Off-strategy initiatives • Efforts ignoring customer research • Executives' pet projects

Source: Adapted in part from *The 7 Habits of Highly Effective People* (New York Free Press, 1989), 149-162.

Finally, if we're grappling with a lack of alignment among executives, we would be smart to take a look at how Amazon's Jeff Bezos thinks about it. He has a leadership principle called "Have a backbone: disagree and commit." I've seen other companies call this "Collaborate and commit." The idea is that leaders need forums to discuss and argue, but it's critical that once a decision is made, everyone must be aligned and show alignment by modeling alignment. "Disagree and fail to commit" is a recipe for dysfunction and exhaustion.

MOVING ON

Overcoming inertia keeps us on track, keeps the energy and focus on the change where and when it's needed. As we'll see in the next chapter, we need to overcome inertia—we need to keep things moving forward—because it's not as easy as simply demanding change from others.

CHAPTER FOUR

- Inertia is an enemy of change. It's not that we're lazy, but we allow many factors to hold back change.
- We let "other stuff" (front-and-center work) get in the way of the long-term visioning we need to do to affect a change.
- New data can distract us; it can make us uncertain and get us to drag our feet.
- A lack of momentum, our lack of urgency, or complacency can cause inertia.
- When we aren't clear and aligned about the change and the end-state, the effort can twist in many directions, exhausting our people.
- An inability for people to digest what's all involved in the change can slow us down.
- Energy slumps happen along the way, and they cause inertia.
- It's important for us to work on the matters that cause our personal inertia, as well as working on the organization's inertia.

FIVE

Enemy #4

Our Belief in Change by Decree

In the early 1980s, the State of Texas found itself dealing with a trash problem. It was spending $20 million a year to clean up litter, and those costs were rising 17 percent per year. There was no end in sight. At this pace, the costs would more than double in just five years. These cost projections were unbearable. (Oh—also—litter is ugly.)

Texas had already tried to change this problem by decree. The legislature had long-before outlawed littering on the state's highways and in public places—just like other states. Signs informing the public that littering was illegal under Texas statutes and that fines would be levied could be seen on highways across the state.

But it didn't stop the behavior. The litter problem kept getting worse. I can imagine that—given how little respect some people had for these litter laws—they likely threw litter *at* the signs, using the legal notice as a target as they sped along the state's highways.

National campaigns had tried to stem the growing litter tide. These were less decrees and more positive campaigns like "Give a hoot, don't pollute," using an owl as the mascot for the campaign. In another campaign, we saw a very sad Native American on a horse, staring out at litter, his mood reflecting how we had littered the land of his ancestors; we saw tears streaming down his face at the end of the ad. I was compelled by it as a boy. But apparently many people were not.

When he became head of the Texas Highway Commission, Bob Lanier learned about this growing financial (and behavioral and environmental) problem. Wanting to cut what he saw as the state's bloated costs across the whole transportation budget, he had examined every line item, and he became focused on this problem in particular.

Lanier asked an ad agency in Austin, GSD&M, to think about a campaign that would combat this growing problem. As advertising executives, the team at GSD&M understood that changing behavior takes more than change by decree; they knew it would require some sort of appeal that hit people in their hearts, not their heads. It had to be something that resonated emotionally with people, something that appealed to their values.

They also knew from research that the biggest litterers were young males in their late teens and early twenties. What would get these young men to change their behavior? What were their values? What would get them to see littering as uncool?

As Texans themselves, these ad execs knew—and they felt—the strong emotional connection Texans have to their state. Texans are darn proud of Texas; schoolchildren pledge allegiance to the state flag after pledging allegiance to the American flag. It's a Texan value to have a swagger when it comes to thinking about their home state.

With all this in mind, the ad execs developed a campaign using a slogan they made up based on Texan values. Instead of suggesting something like "Keep Texas beautiful," they offered: "Don't mess with Texas."

It was rolled out by Texas celebrities such as Stevie Ray Vaughan, who were seen as models to the key demographic. All of this struck an emotional chord with Texans of all ages. It said, "Hey, we're all Texans, and we're proud of that. Let's not trash what we're all proud of." It was a "come with us on this journey" type of statement, even if it was outwardly bold.

The campaign greatly reduced littering. From 1986 to 1991, instead of doubling costs as forecast, littering fell by 70 percent.

Change by decree hadn't worked. Reaching an emotional level in people—especially males of a certain age—appealing to their values, and using role models had changed behavior. And it changed behavior for good. Littering continues to decrease in Texas—it fell another 34 percent from 2009–2013.

CHANGE ON THE CHEAP

If we want our change initiative to be target practice for those who outwardly comply but quietly resist, we'll do well by relying on change by decree.

Change by decree is easy. Senior executives simply decree that the organization is going to do something and—poof—it gets done. Until it doesn't.

Sure, these executives may think they can dress it up with storytelling and whatnot. But it's lazy, and it gets the results it deserves. We eventually have to do it all over again; or we go without the benefits of the change. This is kind of like what my father used to say when I was trying to short-cut something as a kid: "Son, you're working extra hard to make that easy, aren't you?"

The reality is, there's a way to do things, and there's a way not to do things. As we'll discuss later in this chapter, change by decree is out of line with our organization's values—no matter what those values are—and the change we hope for can't be inconsistent with our values, or it simply won't succeed.

Change by decree—especially when it's done all by itself—is an enemy of change. It's change on the cheap. It won't get people to *want* to change. Ironically, change by decree can be necessary, and this can be tricky.

Given market conditions and customer needs, we may be compelled to sell off whole units, downsize, outsource. We may have to reorganize around customer needs because today we're showing our customers our org chart, making them endure the deficiencies of the organization we've built. We may have a crisis, such as a security breach, that requires a change by decree.

But if we want to sustain change in our culture, and even if we're just trying to sustain a change that we made by decree, change by decree—alone—is not reliable. It won't carry the business and the culture forward; it won't change the way the people who stay behind in a downsizing or a spinoff think or feel as employees.

So we have to model the change and give people a voice.

When we're showing our customers our org chart, we can ask our employees (as well as our customers) to help us redesign processes that streamline the customer experience. When we sell off a division, we have to show our sincere concern for those affected (and it has to be sincere... if we don't care, we shouldn't be here). If we have sincere concern, we'll genuinely *do* things that show it: our hearts will inform our actions. When we have a serious security issue, we're very clear why the new way of doing things (often determined quickly without the ability to think everything through) is necessary and what the risks to our enterprise are if we don't comply, but we also ask for feedback on how this new change might be improved in case it's having unforeseen consequences. Model the change and give people a voice.

DON'T BECOME A LAUGHINGSTOCK, PART 1

There's a reason why the movie *Office Space*, the hit TV comedy *The Office*, and the cartoon strip *Dilbert* strike a chord with so many people: there's truth to what goes on there. Art imitates life.

Even though it's more than twenty years old, *Office Space* still packs a punch and continues to have a cult following. I once rewatched it over beers at an off-site event with fellow leaders at a tech company. As we watched it, I looked around the room searching for certain executives to see if they were laughing at particular characters. They were. Some even imitated these characters during the movie.

The funny thing? These people had no idea that the character on the screen was parodying them. Some of the personalities were so spot-on, I thought the filmmakers might have worked at our company. (Of course, none of the characters on the screen could possibly have been parodying me!)

Office Space is set in the late 1990s during the Y2K effort, when technology companies had to reprogram all of their systems, or—when the Year 2000 rolled around—these systems would somehow believe they were reverting back to 1900. This could make the systems inoperable. The movie is full of classic corporate stupidity, and even twenty years ago, the filmmakers used change by decree—layoffs determined by outside consultants—as a gag. The practice has only become more outdated since then.

DON'T BE A LAUGHINGSTOCK, PART 2

So we have art. And now let's take a little time out to make fun of real life!

I've seen plenty of executives make the mistake of thinking that top-down change mechanisms are all that are needed for transformational change. "These people want to resist change? Well, we'll change *their* world!" these executives might say or think. "This'll ensure we get change from *them*."

I imagine we've all seen them. Maybe some of us have even been one. Let's explore my favorite types of top-down execs.

DR. DECREE

There's the executive who thinks he (it's usually a "he" in my experience) can order a transformation, and it will be done. It's not usually as cut and dry as an order from the prison warden in *Shawshank Redemption*—or a blue memo— but the executive tells his team that he wants something changed a certain way, and they scramble to get it done.

In these instances, the executive's cronies will start selling the action with lines like, "Jim wants us to do this," or "We need to do this because Jim's calling for it." (As an ex-crony myself, I now bow in shame for having said things like this earlier in my career.)

If you're Jim, you should know that lines like these are tell-tale signs to everyone that you and your cronies are lazy. You aren't trying to convince people that it's the right thing to do, that it will benefit the enterprise and the people in it. So they shrug their shoulders and hate themselves for complying temporarily.

Maybe the cronies were not brought in on the decision—or they don't much agree with the change. It's not in their hearts, so they aren't going to sell it. They use the executive's name proactively to push things onto people.

Dr. Decree may not even know that his people are carrying out his orders this way. He's surprised when a management consultant tells him about this. But it goes on, and he doesn't necessarily stop this or discourage it.

THE FOOLISH FOISTER

Another example is the executive who comes to a meeting with the change already figured out. He foists his ideas on everyone, starting with his own direct reports. He may act like the team is helping him write the change manifesto, but everyone (except the executive) is the wiser. The executive expects everyone to support this change because "we all came up with it together."

The executive holds a town hall meeting and tells everyone that the company must change because of changing customer needs or competition or new technology. The videos are nice, with great music and people, but the change idea comes from on high and—given that his subordinates don't feel it—their body language and tone tell everyone they aren't fully supportive when they get up onstage to talk about it.

At the first sign of dissent among the troops, given that these subordinates haven't had the chance to think the whole idea through and become one with it (it's not their idea too), they fend off the criticism by telling people, "Well, it was really all Jim's idea," or "You know, Jim really thought such and such was important."

FORCED COMPLIANCE

The reality is, if ordered to, people will comply. The more money or fear we give them, the more intently they'll comply, even if what we've asked them to do causes dissonance.

But it won't stick because we haven't changed beliefs. In fact, a longstanding body of research tells us the more money we give—or pressure we place—to get people to comply, the less likely they are to change their beliefs even though they in fact comply. Social psychologists call this logic-defying phenomenon "forced compliance theory."

Remember, we're *not* trying to change someone who's working an Excel spreadsheet to start using new databases—even if that's the actual outcome we want. Instead, we're trying to change beliefs, we're trying to get them to *want* to change how they work with data, and we're trying to give them reason to believe they need to change how they work. We do this by showing empathy, not edict. We do this by winning over hearts; behaviors will follow. We do this by appealing to our shared values.

VALUES, NOT DECREES

How important are our shared values? Very important.

Thirty years ago, we all heard about organizations' strategic plans. We heard little about values, mission, purpose, and other similar cultural components. Today they're ubiquitous. Employees and potential employees—among others—want to know what kind of character a workplace has, and even how the organization's mission or purpose positively meets societal needs.

In fact, values, mission, purpose, principles, beliefs...these things have become very important to many early and mid-career workers (and even to many late-career people tired of working at places that value only the almighty dollar). Today, values—if they're authentic—can be so ingrained in organizations that they play a fundamental role in decision-making and even the sustainability of our organizations, and we can no longer afford to go off-value.

And change by decree is not aligned with our values. I've never seen an organizational value that reads, "Do as the leader says." This is not North Korea.

In his great book, *It's Not What You Sell, It's What You Stand For*, Roy Spence Jr. puts the focus on what he calls "purpose": why your organization exists—beyond profits. Roy makes the point that organizations that identify their purpose—a calling higher than profits alone—significantly outperform their nonpurposed peers financially.

These purposed organizations make decisions through the prism of their stated purpose, and they're dogmatic about it. They don't rationalize away decisions that would be counter to their purpose; they have the discipline to find ways to thrive within the confines of their purpose.

Perhaps a time when our values are tested most is during change. So whatever behavior we're seeking has to be aligned with our values, the change itself can't be off-value, and change by decree is never aligned with our values.

Instead, we have to model our organization's values if we want our people to digest them and take ownership of them. By being consistent with our values—and reaching people on an emotional level—we can lead, teach, and help people through change.

VALUING LEARNING

We've talked about modeling the change, but we haven't

really discussed modeling values. Values can be abstract, so it's safe to ask, "Can we model values?"

When leaders at a North American financial services organization in the pension and retirement space were concerned their employees were getting stale in their jobs and as an organization, they set out to introduce a change in their own values. The leadership team—after a lot of thought and input from others—decided to add to its stated values the concept of continuous learning. Executives believed that for the organization to survive and even thrive, every member of the team had to be open to constantly growing through learning.

The concept of "failure is not an option" and the idea that we should fear taking risks—these went out the window. After all, failure—if we use it properly by seeing it as a learning opportunity, not a lack of capability on our part—can be a powerful way to learn.

So how did they share this new value of continuous learning with the team? Well, they could have simply added the value to the list on the wall. They could have featured articles on the intranet about the need for continuous learning. They could have added a new online training course on the subject. Or they could have posted signs saying, "Let's all continuously learn!"

These leaders decided to model this new value, this change

in how the organization needed to think going forward. They sought emotional buy-in.

Each quarter at its organization-wide gatherings—largely in its Town Halls—a single member of senior leadership would get on stage alone and give a testimonial about—of all things—a failure of theirs.

They were willing to admit failure. They would share a failure they recently experienced in their own work. They talked about how and when they realized their work was failing. They talked about who they reached out to about this failure—often it was someone they didn't know very well, but they had to go to them, admit they were in trouble, and seek help anyway. They talked about how they turned this project around or pulled the plug on the work.

And they talked about what they personally learned and how they would apply the learnings to their work, to their lives. They talked about how the experience grew them as people and as professionals. They were explicit in tying it back to continuous learning.

This opened the floodgates. People no longer saw failure as—well—failure. They saw it as continuous learning. They weren't failing any more than previously, but the failures that every member suffered from time to time—and, more

importantly, the learning they gained from the experience—
became something to exalt rather than hide.

Far from change by edict, far from foisting a change on
others, these leaders changed their organization and its
values by humbling themselves before their people, they
showed vulnerability when it may have previously been
unsafe, they reached their team on an emotional level,
and they created a learning organization that continues
to thrive today.

RICHER, DEEPER

You have to admit, whether it's "Don't mess with Texas"
and a connection to a place, using a program modeled by
superstar entertainers or promoting a new value by admitting to failure—these are much richer, much deeper ways
for our people to learn the kind of organization we want to
have, the kind of place we want to live in.

It's not as easy as change by decree, but it will have the
opposite effect of forced compliance—people hating themselves while temporarily complying—if we do it right.

And it's light-years different from that company in *Office
Space*, where the boss got up and—trying to singlehandedly render the company "cool"—told his people that Friday
would be Hawaiian shirt day, so everyone could wear jeans!

ACCEPTING A HARD TRUTH

None of us wants to accept that something we already thought would be hard is going to be harder, but we must if we're going to bring about real change. And as we'll see in the next chapter, we also shouldn't make it harder— and less successful at the same time—by focusing on the wrong things.

CHAPTER FIVE

- Change by decree is an enemy of change. It's not in line with our values.
- Change by decree, when we simply tell everyone what the change is with little room for debate, is change on the cheap. It won't get people to *want* to change.
- Ironically, sometimes we have to make changes by decree (such as an acquisition). In these cases, we have to subsequently reach people on an emotional level and get buy-in at many levels on as many aspects as possible related to the post-announcement changes that will come as a result.
- Leaders must authentically help others feel ownership of the change. Our people should have a hand in creating the change if we want them to support the change.
- Our changes must be in alignment with our organization's core values. Core values have become a must for organizations of all stripes, and—given that no organization's values include "Do as the leader says"—change by decree is never congruent with our values.

SIX

Enemy #5

We Live in the Weeds

I once worked with a very data-driven company whose leadership team decided it would do whatever it took to become a best company to work for...one of those top companies listed in _Fortune_ each January. The CEO and his executive team devised a way to do this, and they brought in some of the best and brightest—their high-potential managers, mostly soon-to-be vice presidents—to work on this project for them. Being a best company to work for was very important to them...and to their firm's future.

The people chosen for the project had proven track records in the firm. They were aces at compensation and benefits, finance, marketing analytics, operations sciences. Given that their expertise covered a great range of the organization, they would bring broad insight into what might drive a business like theirs to be rated a best company to work for—and how to track all of this.

This also would be a great way to cross-pollinate the future leaders. People who didn't necessarily know each other well would serve on cross-functional teams for this special project. These very smart, talented people went forth to study all of the top hundred companies on the latest list and visit twenty or so that seemed most like their company.

What would they study? The leadership team wanted data. How much vacation does each firm offer? What's the average compensation for different job types the judges study? Tenure in job for various layers of management. Longevity and turnover. Data about spans and layers. What's in their health benefits packages? How do they track their own progress toward being a best company to work for?

The organization had great expectations. The team back at headquarters built out the grids and formulas they would use to score different variables as they awaited the high-potential teams to come back with their findings.

But when these very talented future leaders came back with their findings, the findings did not compute for those receiving the information.

"You know, it's really about a feeling," they told the leadership team. "These data points we all put together and agreed on—they matter, but only so much. You can't get on the list if you're uncompetitive on these data points. But it's more than that. All of these companies we studied have a different dimension going on that gets them on the list."

I'm told the CEO and others were just shy of pulling their hair out. "A feeling? A different dimension? What the hell is that?" The project ended not long after this. It's been decades now; I look each year, and the company still has not made the ranks of the annual list.

SIMPLICITY IS GENIUS

These leaders were focused on the wrong things. They were focused on the weeds. There are times—it may be often—when a data-driven orientation serves us well. Then there are times when being so data-driven can get in the way of what's really important.

This can be true in business and elsewhere. Take, for example, political campaigns. In his memoir of the 2008 Obama campaign, *The Audacity to Win*, campaign manager David Plouffe writes about the early days of the Democratic primary campaign, which took place in 2007.

Hillary Clinton's campaign, he tells us, had the messaging data and capabilities that a highly sophisticated and well-funded campaign would naturally build—the kind that would be built by experienced, professional presidential campaign leaders. After all, this was how these things work.

Clinton's pollster and messaging guru, Mark Penn, had written a book titled *Microtrends*, and he focused on micro-targeting different populations and precincts with very specific, targeted messages. Plouffe gives us the idea that the Obama campaign believed Clinton's message targeting was precise, down to minute details.

For their part, the Obama campaign, largely newcomers to presidential politics, didn't find this necessary. "We thought this was an election with one big macrotrend—change," Plouffe says.

Obama and his team didn't get tied up in the minutiae that might get in the way of their overarching thinking. They understood that a simple, high-level message would have to work in their campaign. So they kept it simple and pushed their "change" message easily into every conversation, even on complex issues such as diplomacy. They weren't unsophisticated; their heads were just clearer. (Oh, and they won.)

IT'S ABOUT INPUTS

Change programs have been pitched as the equivalent of

political campaigns by some change management consultants. But that's not the connection I'm making here. Nor am I tying Obama's "change" message to this book's theme; that's just a coincidence.

What I'm saying is that, as executives, we have a responsibility to ensure the trains are running on time and in the right direction, but we don't need to know about every working part of each train, each car. We don't have to get so deep into the process—and be so reliant only on data—that we lose sight of what's going to drive the change.

And what's going to drive the change? Inputs. We need to recognize that—now that we're leaders—our jobs are about inputs. Our leverage point is the input; the outcomes will only be as good as the inputs we provide. When we focus so much on outputs—all the nitty-gritty worry when a KPI is red or flipping from green to yellow—it's often too late. We needed to spend our time and focus on the front end of the change effort, priming the change.

When we see problems in our data—in our weeds—we think it's because others aren't doing their jobs, or there's some barrier being created by still others. The reality is, this is a "we" problem; a red KPI can be the outcome of a system or process we built incorrectly somehow. Too often, it's because we haven't primed the change. We're comfortable with data; it's harder to spend our time ripening the atmosphere for the change. A focus on inputs—rather than the weedy data and KPIs and outcomes—will get us the better outcomes we're looking for.

Being in the weeds is yet another enemy of change. It can hold us back from the real work at hand—getting our people to *want* to change.

To be clear, others in the organization do need to focus on and track progress as we accomplish the change or transformation we're all going for, and we should be aware if we're not meeting the goals. Scheduling go dates and then backing into deadlines for earlier targets, mapping resources to ensure they'll be available for every step of the process, understanding why we aren't meeting targets—this work is all essential, but not for us.

It's also essential to keep abreast of milestones because we'll want to overcommunicate the successes the team is having. Momentum is a key factor, as discussed earlier. But the higher up we go in the organization, the less we need to be in the weeds. The weeds only get in the way of our ability to reach people on an emotional level. Weeds keep us from focusing on how we model the change, how we at least act congruently with the change, how we prime our culture for the change.

As we discussed in the introduction, management strategy

heavily emphasizes SMART goals or objectives. Management gurus, project managers and others will tell us to make objectives and goals specific, measurable, achievable, relevant, and timely.

It's valid advice. Without specifics, the organization can wander aimlessly, exhausting our people in the process. Without measurability, there is no accountability. Achievability makes it worth trying, lest our team be overwhelmed or discouraged by something unachievable. By being relevant, we can all see how it ties in logically to the big picture. And timelines also create accountability, plus a sense of urgency.

Discipline for the process can't be discounted, and setting goals *is* an input.

NEW FINDINGS

But science tells us it can't be just about SMART—the logical, rational side of things.

When we're going through a change, logic and discipline—as important as they are—must often be secondary, especially the higher up we are. All the nitty-gritty weedy worry about performance indicators, all the weedy focus on metrics and timelines—none of it has relevance if our people aren't with us from the start. Those green and yellow dots will turn red if we aren't thinking about emotions.

How do we know the importance of heart, of emotion?

We Need Both Heart and SMART Change

SMART Change Involves	Heart Change Involves
• Project management	• Striking an emotional chord
• Technology timelines	• Pulling for the change, not forcing it
• Business strategy	• Modeling/acting congruently
• Finance (capitalization, costs)	• Inviting input from others
• Implementation	• Transparency
• Training	• Smart patience with people
• Work environment plans	• Communications through actions
• Traditional communications	• Going slow to go fast

For a century or more, the scientific community concluded that good decisions were made only rationally—"He's just letting his emotions get in the way," someone might say if a friend seemed to act irrationally. But the past two decades have brought us a growing body of science, particularly with the emergence of new findings in the age of technology, such as magnetic resonant imaging, and it's teaching us the importance of emotion in decision-making—even rational decision-making.

In the 1990s in his laboratory at the University of Iowa, Antonio Damasio and a team of neuroscientists launched what has become a revolution in neuroscience, showing us that without the work of the brain's emotional capabilities, people can't make the simplest of rational decisions. He describes patients with a damaged amygdala, hippocampus, or other areas of the limbic system—the parts of the brain that are needed to process emotion—and these patients' inability to make the simplest of decisions, such as the choice of a restaurant.

"Well, we could go to this one," Damasio says, imitating a research subject. "But I take it that this restaurant has been rather empty recently, so that's probably a bad sign, a sign that the food may not be so good. On the other hand, it's true that if it is more empty, we are likely to get a table. Therefore, we should go there."

"The thing would go on endlessly," he says, "and you really feel like pounding on the table and saying, 'Get real.'

"The reason why they can't choose is that they haven't got this sort of lift that comes from emotion. Emotion allows you to mark things as good, bad, or indifferent."

Damasio, now at the University of Southern California and the author of the groundbreaking *Descartes' Error,* explains that past emotional reactions teach us whether we like something. Our brains mark past decisions not only by how they came out rationally—whether they were good or bad for us in business or life—but also by the emotions that resulted when we made these decisions—whether we felt good or bad at the time.

We pocket these historic decision markers in our brains and

use them for future decisions that become simple for us. As a three-year-old, if we're told not to touch something hot—like a stove burner—and we touch it anyway, we remember rationally that it hurt, and we consolidate this memory with our emotional memory that it upset us. Our brain packages this into a decision marker that tells us to stay away from hot things, and we use that packaged marker for the future (it sits in our brains forever, provided the area where it's stored is not injured). Even patients with amnesia retain these markers and can use them.

But in people who later lose the use of the emotion-processing parts of the brain, they cannot make new decision packages or markers. And they can't even make the simplest of rational decisions.

Let's test this against the heart and SMART analogy.

With science telling us for a century that our rational brains alone make our decisions, it made complete sense for change management and many other business and societal disciplines to focus solely on the rational. But with the growing knowledge that our emotional selves are central to even the smallest rational decisions, emotion cannot be discounted.

"It's not that we are saying that reason is not important and that knowledge and logic are not important," Damasio says, but "you cannot have normal decision-making without the emotion factors.

"Intelligent decision-making is impossible without emotion, because emotion marks the value and draws you toward one decision or another."

So our people—like all people—need an emotional component to their rational decisions.

When we ask our people to rationally decide that change is in their—and the organization's—best interest, and we fail to include emotional markers for this decision-making, we leave them to set their own emotional markers, markers that can bring about rational decisions that are either supportive or hurtful to our change efforts. By offering emotional considerations that are congruent with the change, we're helping them make rational decisions in line with our change efforts; we're helping them decide to come with us on the change journey.

And the time to do it is on the front end of change—the inputs—not once a green KPI has turned yellow.

BUT HOW DO I MEASURE HEART?

SMART is a widely used standard for deciding how to manage change. More than any other part of the term, the

M (measurable) influences why we focus on the intellectual aspects of managing change and put less emphasis on the emotional aspects.

As I was writing this book, a good friend—an engineer by training—asked me this question: "But how do I measure 'heart'? I mean, that's the only way we can ensure anything gets done, by measuring it." He was very concerned about this.

There are, of course, ways to measure the emotional connection employees have to an organization. Engagement surveys are a tried and true way to do it. But most—if not all—of these tools are annual...certainly not daily or monthly or even quarterly. Quick pulsing surveys can help us some, but they don't give us the same data and measurement rigor of a full engagement survey. So, for all practical purposes, there is no red, yellow, and green way to update heart and its KPI for a smaller given time. Focus groups, roundtables, and other shorter-term ways of gathering insight provide anecdotal insights, not hard data.

We may be able to infer "heart"—or lack thereof—by looking at our own KPI measurements, seeing what things are running smoothly and where things are slow. Perhaps some teams are throwing up logical, smart-seeming reasons for not acting, and we may dig into it and find that those with all the "not-to" reasons have decided just to be confused while the people who are running things smoothly are so bought-in that they're working weekends without a second thought.

One emotion that can be causing this is simple fear; we know it can get in the way of action, and if we smell that fear is present, we need to build confidence by showing the way, by listening and encouraging, not by creating more fear (even if our patience may be running out). Ideally, though, we would be building confidence as an input, not a remediation.

The challenge here, in the end, is twofold: heart is an input, not a result, so it's much harder to see. One seasoned change consultant tells me: "Most of the success will be anecdotal at first. You just have to live with that."

Second—and this will make some people want to throw this book away—there are actually some things that are important to our work that can't be measured. This may be hard to accept, and many may debate it, but—given that heart is an *input*, not an output—I'm willing to posit that we can't always measure exactly how much "heart" is going into a project.

Remember, what have all the measurable, nonheart books, research, and practices on change management brought us? Just a two-thirds failure rate.

As they say, it's a feeling.

HOW TO GET OUT OF THE WEEDS

RECOGNIZE AT THE BEGINNING OF THE CHANGE THAT IT'S ABOUT INPUTS

We need to prime the change with an emotional atmosphere that gets our team accepting and ready for the change. We'll see in later chapters how to do this. Know why we need the change and be consistent in explaining it; involve and listen to our people's ideas for how to address the change; and be true to our values when determining how we'll change.

CLEAR MESSAGING

We can't let the weeds complicate our messaging. We need consistent, simple, and clear explanations of why the change is necessary, what it means for each group. We shouldn't overburden people with nongermane facts. We need to model the change. And we must speak with one voice. We'll also talk about this later.

In addition, we need to make prioritization and expectations clear. We must make the SMART part—the execution—simple for people, step-by-step if possible.

REMEMBER LESS

We must avoid getting bogged down by complicated formulas for success. On my journey researching change thinking,

I've come across all kinds of suggestions—many of them complicated. We need to look out for these overly complicated approaches that make us memorize 23 of this and 15 of that. They'll keep us in the weeds.

Some books and articles act as sort of workbooks for the change team to reference when planning for and developing change plans. This makes sense. As a frontline manager of people—or even higher up in the organization—it may be prudent to keep a handy reference on what we need to do. But for every good workbook, there's the book with 191 things to remember.

We can't remember all of this stuff when coming across hairy problems within our change efforts. But we can remember this: we have to *exhibit* the change if we ever have a chance to get our people to *want* to change, and our best impact is in the inputs, not the outcomes.

That's why this book is not about what we do as much as it's about the spirit with which we do it. I'm offering a different dimension to lift change programs—something that will keep our heads above water even as we have to focus on some of the fundamentals of our change program and its progress.

HEARTS, NOT WEEDS

Bottom line: we can't automate change. Without the hearts of our people, we have little chance of getting them to *want* to do anything specific, measurable, achievable, relevant, or timely anytime soon. We'll see some greens, some progress, but they'll revert back to yellows and reds if we haven't built sustainable emotional buy-in among the team first.

So let's get out of the weeds. The weeds may be our comfort zone. They may be what makes us successful in regular time. But this is a time when we need people to change... when we need people to *want* to change.

Focus on people. Get into their hearts. Do it from the start. This will make the SMART work, work. And as we'll see in our next chapter, we need to understand our people and where they're coming from if we're ever going to get into their hearts with our change.

CHAPTER SIX

- Being in the weeds is an enemy of change.
- As leaders, we need to ensure the trains are running and headed in the right direction, but we don't need to know every aspect of how the trains run.
- We need to track milestones, understand what things are going wrong and right. Our efforts must be SMART (specific, measurable, achievable, relevant, and timely).
- But much of the red, yellow, and green directional outcomes are dependent on whether our people *want* to change.
- This requires reaching people emotionally, not just rationally, from the start. Great outcomes come from great inputs, so we need to focus on the right inputs.
- New science tells us that people can't make rational decisions without the help of the brain's emotional processors.
- If we don't reach our people on an emotional level, our people will certainly decide on their own how to fill the emotional part of the decisions they must make.
- Modeling change is a very good way to reach people on an emotional level and gives them a model to follow through the change.

SEVEN

Enemy #6

How We View People

A peer of mine was complaining to me one afternoon. "This would be a great place to work, and we could get a lot done, if only we didn't have people working here."

He was joking, of course, but we had just had a terrifically dreadful experience trying to convince some people about a change we were trying to introduce. Arms were folded. Lots of long stares at us. Not much participation. Very uncomfortable.

The reality is we need people to make change happen. Their ability and willingness to change—their *want* to change—is the difference between enduring success and failure. But we often don't decipher how to deal with different types of people, and we let this get in the way of the change. If we don't try to understand them and grow ourselves to match up with their needs, people—and how we view them—can be an enemy of change.

The WANT to Change

Getting people to change behaviors	Getting people to *want* to change behaviors
• Pushing change • Decreeing change • Incentivizing change ($$) • Using fear	• Pulling for change • Modeling the hoped-for change • Reaching them on an emotional level • Tying the change to our core values
RESULTS	**RESULTS**
• Compliance for now • Less likely changed beliefs	• Contagion among teammates • Changed beliefs • More likely lasting change

We have to recognize that some people are cut out for change, and others just aren't. We need to understand the difference. And at some point—especially once we've tried all of our best efforts, once we've listened to them and modeled the change for them—we have to decide how much of our limited time and energy we can afford to invest in those who simply can't change. As Jim Collins, in his important book, *Good To Great*, so artfully teaches, if we don't get the right people on the bus and the wrong people off the bus, we can doom our efforts.

Ultimately, if we really want the change, we may very well have to let some people go—even some of our closest leaders. This is hard, and we have to always embody dignity and respect, but we owe some decisiveness to those who will remain, and taking this kind of action is—in itself—communicating the importance of the change. Ron Williams, who successfully led Aetna through a massive transformation, now looks back on his work and says perhaps his biggest regret is that he didn't make personnel decisions sooner; he was empathetic (a good thing), but it meant that he sometimes tried too long and too hard. I've heard this from countless other leaders.

So how should we look at people? I admire the work that Marsha Clark—the former EDS executive and current management practitioner (not the former prosecutor)—has done, capturing five categories people fall into during change events. I've shamelessly adopted her five categories and then added my thoughts on how to understand them, as well as keys to leading them through the change process.

THE "IT'S ABOUT TIME" PEOPLE

When we tell them about a change initiative, these people might say, "What the hell have we been waiting for?" Not only did they see the big picture—the macro trends, competitive pressures, changing customer needs, lack of internal engagement—as early or earlier than us, but now that it's been announced, they can't wait for the change to happen. There are two things to do about these people:

- Love them. Get them as engaged as possible in the change effort. Listen and seek their ideas from the start because these people already have ownership of what needs to be changed (it was their idea, after all), now it's time to help them usher in the future state. We can do this by asking them what they would do (they'll have ideas) and bounce our ideas off of them. They'll feel engaged if we listen to them, hear them out, and (hopefully) harness their ideas. Think about how they can become a greater part of the change—ambassadors, kitchen cabinet members.
- Be thoughtful about them. Some of them may think they're smarter than us because they saw the need for change before we announced it. They may be back-channeling their smartness—and our slowness—to others. We can't let this get in the way. This is about successfully changing things, not about who's smart or our feelings. Salute them for being ahead of the curve, let it be their idea. Engage them. Make the fact that they already had the idea a potent part of their recruitment as ambassadors, kitchen cabinet members, or simply as the people who will make the change happen in every-day terms.

THE POLITICALLY CORRECT

These people will say all the right things but largely not do any of the right things. They may be passive-aggressive for at least a couple of reasons:

- They're under extraordinary pressure to produce in the here and now, and this requires that they use today's systems and processes to get things done. So while they need to survive politically, they also fear they'll be fired if they let the team down in the near term. We should start by listening to discern if this is indeed their challenge. And if it is, we need to inject ourselves and help them balance the change with the here and now. They also need to see that the change effort is serious and not going away. Given that communications is 90 percent action and 10 percent words, this is also where modeling the change—changing ourselves to show them the serious nature and permanence of the change—will tell them the change is unavoidable. This will help them come to their own conclusion that they need to figure out how to balance things during the transition.
- Less likely, they're duplicitous and really don't want to change. We have to determine if these people are causing enough distraction and taking enough away from the change effort to keep them around.

THE "BUT I NEED MORE INFORMATION" PEOPLE

During a change effort, people can be as confused as they allow themselves to be; cognitive dissonance can drag them down. But we shouldn't assume they're confused (or need more information) by choice or that they're hopeless. Here are a couple of takes on them:

- They may be earnestly trying to envision the future state without all the skills to do it. We won't have all the answers to their questions, but we should understand that some people are less able to process ambiguity than others. There's really a two-pronged approach to take with them. First, it's on us to paint as clear a directional picture of the future as possible, using principles as our guideposts. For example, if the principle is about becoming much more customer-centric after years of organizational centricity, we can help them understand how to choose the more customer-centric approach when they get to a fork in the road. Practice makes better in these cases. Second, we can show them the way. By modeling what a more customer-centric manager looks like—for example, telling good and bad stories about the forks we've faced in our own customer-centricity journey and how we handled them—we can help them become more comfortable with the new reality, even if there's still ambiguity involved.
- Or perhaps they're overwhelmed by cognitive dissonance and—given their comfort with the old ways—they're drowning. If the process above doesn't work for them, we have to decide how much additional investment they're worth. Could their talents be used elsewhere in the organization? Patience is a virtue... until it's not.

THE "BUT I'M TRYING" PEOPLE

Like the "But I Need More Information" people, these are people who sincerely may be trying to understand the new way, but—in their case—they lack confidence. Building confidence in those who lack it is both possible and laudable, and it takes a lot of baby steps sometimes. This is where storytelling can be crucial. This is about talking up successes elsewhere in the organization, or even successes at other organizations that have tried the same thing. "If they can do it, we can certainly do it. I know we can."

THE "I'M NOT GOING" PEOPLE

People who are verbal about their opposition to the change are cancers. Like weeds among crops—which suck up an inordinate amount of water and minerals and are more likely to frustrate photosynthesis by blocking sunlight with their larger leaves—these people need to be pulled out of the garden, roots and all. Otherwise, they'll kill the change if we let them stay. Firing people who are outspoken opponents is an action. Actions speak.

MAKING THEM "NOW I SEE IT" PEOPLE

In all of these cases, storytelling is a very effective way to help our people see what we're seeing and make our ideas contagious. We need to share examples of people who faced the same challenges (inside our own organization or elsewhere) so they gain the confidence that it can be done. Examples of customer pain give our people context that can open their eyes to the need for change. Examples of successful changes at other organizations (or other parts of our organization) can help our people gain confidence.

Another way to get people to rally around change is to reach them on a sensory level. As I mentioned with two stories in Chapter 1 about Martin (with the room arranged to tell me, "This is important") and John Stegner (the gloves stacked on the boardroom table), our senses—smell, touch, taste, sight, and hearing—are powerful teaching tools.

And still another way to build momentum is called "tipping-point" change, where some people rally around the change, energizing others to rally around it, which gets others into it, until we reach a tipping point.

This can move the "politically correct" people or the "I need more information" people to become "oh, now I see it" people. And these concepts—storytelling, sensory experiences, and tipping-point change—were key teaching tools when William Bratton got his lieutenants back underground.

Bratton is one of the most recognized and successful American police leaders in modern times. He led the New York Police Department twice, ran the Los Angeles Police Department for seven years and, earlier in his career, led the Boston Police Department. In all three cities, he turned around departments that were suffering from morale problems and/or controversy, and his efforts have drastically lowered crime rates.

Bratton is probably best known for bringing to life a policing model developed earlier by criminal justice experts he worked with, known as the "broken windows theory." This espouses that visible signs of disorder, even for less injurious crimes—vandalism, graffiti, vice, broken windows—encourage more serious crimes in a neighborhood.

Bratton is less known for his four years (1990–1994) at the New York Transit Police Department, which he headed just before his first stint leading the NYPD. His time there included a lesson in how a leader can model behavior to teach others. By teaching his subordinates through his stories and actions—and getting them to see, feel, hear, and smell what he was experiencing—he was able to get them just as engaged in and excited about the change, allowing for a tipping point.

When he took the reins at the Transit Police, his subordinates prided themselves on the fact that only 3 percent of serious crime took place in the city's subway system. They monitored crime rates at different subway stops, focusing on response times and—in a few instances—crimes prevented. But given that serious crime was so low in the transit system, there was little need for drastic change in how policing was done there. Or so the leaders of the department thought.

Each morning, these leaders drove to work in department-issued cars. They moved around the city in their department-provided cars. And, given that many of them lived outside the city and its subway system, they headed home at night in the same department-owned cars. Their days largely did not involve going underground.

By contrast, Bratton, who had just moved from Boston and was living in the heart of the city, exclusively used public transit to get around. Riding the subway, he was hit by what riders were experiencing. He saw the filth. He couldn't avoid the horrible smells of urine and other odors left by the estimated 5,000 homeless people who lived in the system; almost every train car seemed to be the dwelling place of at least one homeless person. He witnessed on a daily basis the fare evasion and the broken turnstiles. When I interviewed him for this book, he said he now looks back on that time and likens the subways to hell. "It was like Dante's *Inferno*."

He also saw how subway riders felt. "They were scared to death," he recalls. "They were angry. They were frustrated. There were dozens of track fires because of all the litter in the subway. They were aggravated going into the dirty subway stations where half the lights weren't working."

By taking the subway, he quickly came up to speed on what was really going on at that time in the subway system—aside from the statistics and war stories he heard from others in the department. At nights, he would literally get lost in the subway.

"I loved it when a train door would open and I'd step on the platform. There'd be a cop there on the platform, and he'd see me, and I'd just surprise the hell out of him," he recalls. "Here was the chief at three o'clock in the morning. I was just wandering around trying to learn what it was like to be a transit cop in a subway station."

Talking to cops, Bratton also learned firsthand about the tough working conditions and low morale the police force was facing.

Word spread among his subordinates, and Bratton started sharing with them—using simple storytelling—what he was experiencing. It's never good to know less than your boss, so this encouraged these subordinates to get down into the subway like Bratton. They started riding the subway across town and visiting stations and locker rooms. This put more cops in the system—visible to both the public and station police, who were stretched very thin.

Many of these senior leaders had rarely ridden the subway for years. By following Bratton's modeling, they came face to face with reality. They smelled the urine and trash and other odors of the homeless. They saw the filth firsthand. They felt what it was like to be panhandled regularly. They couldn't deny the problems facing their subordinates.

"My guys once again got intimate with the system, and with that intimacy, they began advocating for their cops better," he says. "They were also much better positioned to strategize when we'd have our executive sessions about how to start fixing the problems. I could count on their collective knowledge built up over the years."

This experience revived the department's sense of urgency. These senior leaders *wanted* change. They brought rich ideas, ideas that increased the police force's visibility among riders and criminals, ideas that solved issues such as the long processing times and lack of transportation for getting criminals through the processing system. Bandwidth improved, arrests increased, and people saw it was happening.

"The cops are back," Bratton would tell the city. In his four years running the transit police, crime dropped dramatically. And it has remained low; subway crime rates for overall crime and even major crimes are down more than 90 percent from their 1990 levels.

Modeling the behavior by taking the subway himself and

sharing his experiences through storytelling gave his subordinates the pull they needed to follow his example. It opened their senses to what was really happening in the system, and this brought about a very different future for the subway. It tipped things against crime and in favor of order.

Modeling was clearly part of Bratton's success, and he had similar success in all the cities where he served, leading to similar benefits. In fact, Bratton's record overall has been remarkable, and his practices have been copied by police forces throughout the US and around the world.

IT COMES BACK TO MODELING

Bottom line: when people are getting in the way of change, it's on us to see if we can help them understand what we want—or don't want—by modeling change in a way that uses their human senses to get the change. We need to start by giving them the benefit of the doubt, even if they look like they seem politically correct or underinformed. We need to share stories that inspire them to act differently.

As we'll see in the next chapter, we need to pull them through the change, just as Bratton did.

CHAPTER SEVEN

- If we fail to understand our people and what to do about them, they can be an enemy of change.
- Some people are ready for the change before we are. We should get them to help us.
- Some people are too burdened with current processes to switch to new ones. We need to help them with the transition, including by modeling.
- Others can't handle ambiguity. We need to help them by setting a clear vision, showing them the way, and patiently answering their questions—as long as we can.
- Some lack confidence. Building confidence in people is important and laudable, but we must also keep an eye on where our time investments are best made.
- Some people act duplicitously. No matter what job they have, they need to be fired, or they will continue to undermine the change.

Part Two

How We Become the Allies of Change

EIGHT

Reorientation

We Pull. We Don't Push

What is it about successful change leaders—those who modeled the change—that makes them stand apart from those whose efforts failed? Is there an underlying mindset that drove them to act this way?

These were the questions I asked myself again and again as I pored over my notes and reflected on my interviews and on the many change efforts I'd seen and been a part of—both successful and unsuccessful.

All of the successful change leaders I'd interviewed, worked with, and researched had different styles. They were at different levels in their organizations when the changes they championed took place. Their backgrounds and how they got to their roles were different. They were in different organizations at different organizational life stages, and they each needed their change for different reasons.

Despite all these differences, I sensed that a thread ran through their motivations that might make easy sense of why they succeeded. Was there something about how they approached their change initiatives—before they ever had the idea to model the change in a certain way—something before their simple actions, something that set them apart from other leaders and other leadership techniques? If so, how could I explain this?

Then, by chance, one Saturday morning, I was looking at my Twitter feed, and someone was celebrating the anniversary of the 1920 London Olympics. The tweet included film footage from back in the day: a man on the horizontal bars, for example, and footage of tug-of-war. The fact that tug-of-war was ever an Olympic sport was news to me, I thought, as I watched two teams pulling, pulling, pulling.

That afternoon as I was driving home from the gym, things suddenly clicked. "They were all pulling," I told myself. "They all pulled!"

These successful leaders pulled their people through the change. They set the example. They didn't tell people—push people—to do it; instead, they encouraged and inspired people by their own actions, and their people came along.

IMAGINE YOUR LEADER, ALONE

Imagine for a moment a tug-of-war is taking place, and you stumble upon it. Your boss, your leader, is alone, pulling the rope for you and your organization. He or she is getting pulled pretty hard because there are five people on the other side pulling in the other direction. They're your competitors. Are you going to sit there and let your leader and your organization be humiliated by the other team, or are you—provided you have the physical ability—going to run over and grab the rope behind him or her?

Obviously, the answer is that you'd grab the rope—and it's very likely you'd do so with great purpose and intent. You'd even yell to other coworkers to come join you. If you have a competitive bone in your body, you simply would not let this stand. You can see that the threat is immediate; you see your boss is pulling the best he can, but he's no Superman; and you want to help—you want to win. And you came to this conclusion on your own; it was your idea.

Compare this scene to another tug-of-war. There are five people ready to pull on your competitor's side, and no one is on your side of the rope. Your leader is standing there looking out at the team.

He's saying, "Who should we get to fight this battle for us?"

After discussing with his leadership team, he says "OK, I'd

like the following people to line up at the rope and pull for our team."

He and his leaders then sit nearby and track the effort, calling out ideas to those pulling, giving technical advice, and even offering criticism in an effort to help.

If your name were to be called, how would you feel about it? You'd comply. And I'm sure you'd want to win. I'd also bet you'd feel like if you didn't win, everyone would be looking at you and your teammates as the reason why your organization didn't win, so your motivation would be not to lose; it would be less about winning one for the team and the boss and the organization—especially if you're being critiqued by your bosses. Would you have the same resolve and purpose if you were told to do it? I doubt it, and I'll bet you doubt it too.

This is the difference between being told to do something—being pushed—and deciding to do it for yourself. One is compliant. The other is contagious...with you *wanting* to join and encourage others.

PULL FOR SUCCESS

There are plenty of times when bosses need to push and when pushing is really the only way of managing some situations. Deadline-driven work and immediate safety and security issues require push. Crisis situations usually call for push leadership; there's usually no time in a crisis to inspire people to do things. We all just have to do them.

But for successful, enduring change initiatives, my research and experience are clear: we have to pull. Pulling is about inspiring people to follow us, building infectiousness to what we're doing, engaging people's emotions and senses, and touching people's feelings.

It's about making something their idea—at least in part. We can't expect enduring change—change that's owned by the whole group—to come out of something that's forced on people and done for distant reasons. Pushing is our (the executives') idea; it's from above. Pulling creates something within. It's about getting our people primed for change—rather than micromanaging how something gets executed. Enduring change—a want to change—comes when we pull them first, then we let them take us the rest of the way.

Think about the leaders we've learned about already:

- When Michelle Peluso was leading Travelocity, and the customer service team was unconvinced about the massive change Michelle and her team were leading, she pulled them through to become believers in "customer championship" by showing them how serious she was. She put her money where her mouth was.

- When William Bratton needed to change the attitudes of the transit police, he didn't push them to change their attitudes or institute the changes. He encouraged them—by his actions—to experience riding the subway regularly once again, and they concluded for themselves that they needed to drive a major overhaul.
- The furniture executive we studied didn't succeed by telling people—pushing people—to use the collaboration space at his headquarters. He pulled them; he gave them permission to behave how he hoped they would. They followed.
- The State of Texas, for decades, tried to push people to stop littering by threatening fines. Only when they pulled people—reached them on an emotional level by appealing to their pride in their home state—did they accomplish change.
- The leaders of the financial services company we studied didn't push people to engage in continuous learning; they pulled people to engage in learning, doing so by example, by admitting their own failures and telling their team what they learned from them.

IRONY?

This is a reorientation for most of us because it's ironic. Often, our default thinking is that bosses tell people what to do. They push; they don't pull.

Telling people what to do was, in fact, largely central to managing for a very long time, possibly since the beginning of time. And we grow up with this impression. When asked what the boss does, kids don't say, "The boss is the motivator in chief who gets people to follow him through thick and thin." To kids, the boss is the person who tells other people what to do.

This idea of the boss gets reinforced again and again. Our parents tell us they're the boss. In school, our teachers and then our professors are the bosses of the classroom, doling out assignments and determining grades. As we begin our careers, we still need supervision. And even though we get more autonomy as we gain expertise, we still get orders from our superiors from time to time, especially during trying times.

Push is also more obvious to us, more memorable. We remember when our boss tells us to do something; it's not always pleasant, and it doesn't inspire the creative juices.

But when we get pulled, we may not even be aware someone's pulling us because it seems natural to be going in that direction. Pulling makes us feel like it was our idea. So we remember when we're pushed; we may not remember when we're pulled.

When it comes to change initiatives, we—managers of

people, all the way up to the CEO—need to pull. And we need to be visible about it...we need to make it as memorable as we can.

But this is hard, in part, because we often don't start change initiatives until we're already behind the curve. Maybe our competitor has cut into our market share using business model innovation. Or a new technology is disrupting our industry. Crime has overtaken our city. We need to differentiate ourselves better to defend our brand in the market. Our stakeholders—shareholders, board members, other investors, bosses, citizens, the media—they're tearing into us about this.

By the time it's time to change, we're often at a DEFCON level known as "hair on fire." There's an existential threat out there; someone or something is going to kill us if we don't act.

We're naturally thinking, "We need to change fast. How do we get our people to change?" "Get" our people to change... that's thinking in terms of pushing for change, not pulling.

So do we really have the time and patience to pull, to inspire, to create infectiousness for what needs to get done? It probably doesn't feel like it.

PULL NEVERTHELESS

It couldn't have felt like it for a leader named Daniel when he was trying to convince his team to focus on the internet in 1998. But he pulled, nonetheless.

After finishing law school, Daniel in 1985 had taken $5,000 he'd saved while delivering pizzas and started a mortgage lending firm in the Detroit area called Rock Financial. During the next thirteen years, he and his team built Rock Financial into a large midwestern brick-and-mortar lender.

But by 1998, Daniel was concerned that a new, disruptive medium known as the internet would take hold in his industry, and he desperately reached out to his entire team to build excitement and solicit ideas. It's clear in the email that kicked off the effort (which I have included below in its entirety, jargon and all) that he pulls. He pulls desperately, eagerly, excitedly, but he pulls.

Everybody,

Below you will find an extremely enlightening and surprising story about Internet mortgages.

I believe we are drastically behind in this very important medium. Ironically, it is Rock Financial that is probably ahead in all other "front end" origination technology, especially with the recent laptop/DU/Lakewood integration project.

We MUST take this great technology to the Internet.

Can you imagine thousands of people in 50 states applying online literally getting a "DU TYPE" full-blown approval in two minutes and then having all of their data downloaded to our Lakewood system?

At the same time, we get their credit card deposit online as well as execute vendor orders instantaneously. In addition, their rate is locked and our "fulfillment center" is notified to execute an extremely simplified version of MIAB (or should I say Approval In A Box).

We also have our call center staffed with experts who can answer any Internet customer's call and questions (hopefully while they are simultaneously looking at the same screen as Mr. Borrower is viewing). The borrower would literally "take his own app," give us his credit card deposit, lock his own loan and by applying, order his own vendor items.

The marketing ideas that would drive people to our site are endless and boundless. I have visited most mortgage sites. NOBODY has anything like I am describing YET. Somebody will. Who will it be? I'll tell you this, whoever it is will WIN BIG!!!!!!!!!!!!!!!!

I am willing to spend as much money to make this happen as is needed to get this true REVOLUTION going.

I would even be willing to purchase a local web development company to make this happen ASAP. That approach would give us several experts who could work full time on getting up and maintaining our site. We already have the technology to make this happen. I believe it is about employing enough of the right human capital NOW that will establish us as a premier national online mortgage organization. This is a wakeup call, everybody. There has never been a greater and more efficient way to pump our origination numbers up to the sky, and at the same time have costs associated with it at minuscule levels compared with what you would have to spend today.

Let's change the mortgage world forever.

Please give me all of your feedback immediately and then I will call an "Internet revolution summit" sometime this week. This is a race. Are you ready to run as hard as ever to win it?

See you at the finish line.

—Dan G.

It's hard to argue that Daniel wasn't successful in this pull effort. His people made his vision a reality. And, long story short, twenty-plus years later, Rock Financial is now known as Quicken Loans, and Daniel—Dan Gilbert—still the company's leader, is the billionaire owner of the Cleveland

Cavaliers, among countless other ventures. Not only has Quicken Loans surpassed Wells Fargo as the largest mortgage lender in the US, but it's also won countless awards, including J.D. Power awards for customer satisfaction, and it's regularly rated a best company to work for.

How did he do it? He could have been a complete task master, calling a meeting and parceling out orders, bludgeoning people. This would have been top-down change management. But as intense as Dan is said to be, and as heated as 1998 was for internet land grabs in every industry imaginable, he still knew he had to pull. He's from Detroit, but this was no blue memo.

Let's look at some of the language Dan used because it comes from a place of pulling not pushing. And that place—that attitude—can't be faked.

He's definitely "hair on fire" about this, and he uses what's going on at the time (internet disruption) to galvanize his people.

Words like "NOW" in all caps, "ASAP," and statements like "NOBODY has anything like I am describing YET. Somebody will." and "This is a wakeup call, everybody."—all of this builds a sense of urgency, it draws on his people's competitive spirit.

Although he says his team is behind, he quickly brings hope and calls some of Rock Financial's current technology "great."

> "Ironically...Rock Financial...is probably ahead in all other 'front end' origination technology, especially with the recent... integration project. We MUST take this great technology to the Internet."

He paints an exciting vision for how things can be.

> "Can you imagine thousands of people in 50 states applying online literally getting a...full-blown approval in two minutes and then having all of their data downloaded to our Lakewood system?"

> "The borrower would literally 'take his own app,' give us his credit card deposit, lock his own loan and by applying, order his own vendor items."

> "The marketing ideas that would drive people to our site are endless and boundless."

He models by telling his team he'll do what it takes to win... he's all-in.

> "I am willing to spend as much money to make this happen as is needed to get this true REVOLUTION going. I would even

be willing to purchase a local web development company to make this happen ASAP."

He ends with a "come with me" message, not a "you will do this" message.

"Let's change the mortgage world forever."

"There has never been a greater and more efficient way to pump our origination numbers up to the sky, and at the same time have costs associated with it at minuscule levels compared with what you would have to spend today."

He invites his people to join the effort, and he wants to listen.

"Please give me all of your feedback immediately."

"This is a race. Are you ready to run as hard as ever to win it?"

"See you at the finish line."

There's something else about Dan Gilbert that speaks to pulling. He doesn't outsource the culture stuff. Not only has he built a powerful culture that uses isms—beliefs such as "Yes before no" and "Simplicity is genius"—but he also takes time out of his very busy schedule—full of quadrant I stuff, to be sure—to teach every orientation class at his growing list of companies. Clearly, he understands the idea of pulling—and its connection to modeling. He understands that people will pull—if we ask them to pull with us.

PULLING VS. MODELING

You may be wondering, "Aren't 'modeling' and 'pulling' the same thing? Or how do they fit with one another?" I spent a good bit of time thinking about this—I considered calling it all "modeling"—but they're different, and one can lead to the other.

Modeling is action. It's the act of holding all our one-on-one meetings in a social space. It's using side-by-side computer monitors in our law office instead of having paper all about.

Pull is more mindset. It's about "come with me." It's about recognizing that we can't manage change by edict and instead that we have to help our people believe in the change and get them to take ownership of it. It's the belief set that influences us to not be the traditional boss...the one who orders people to do things. It's the mindset that influences us to model.

In fact, we're less likely to even think of modeling if we have a mindset of pushing. And if modeling does happen without a pull mindset, it's more likely to be empty, looking contrived. ("I heard I have to model it, so here I am. Look at me, let me communicate it to everyone, and then I'll be glad I'm done with it." We'll talk about avoiding this kind of cheesy communication [in actions and words] in the final chapter.)

Dan Gilbert didn't tell his people, "We are all going to the internet, and it will be great"; he essentially said, "Come to the internet with me, and I'm so excited about this that I had a thought: I'll even buy a local web development company and invest whatever it takes." He modeled as a result of his pull mindset.

IT POINTS TO PULLING

So if we want people to change, if we want lasting change, we have to do it from a mindset of pulling. We have to do this stuff right.

I'm sure someone will claim otherwise, but I can't find one example of successful, enduring change that happened through pushing. They all happened when some sort of pull was involved.

And remember, two-thirds of change efforts fail. Do we really want to fail by pushing and then find ourselves even further behind the curve?

What I will lay out in this part of the book is a process that will allow us and leaders at every level to successfully pull, to model the change, or at least be congruent with the change. Leaders have to collectively believe in—and agree on—what the problem is. Then we have to recognize we don't have all the answers, so we must listen. This way, everyone believes in and has a stake in the change. And only then can leaders at every level model the change...only then can we effectively pull.

This section is the hard part of the book—where the rubber meets the road—but I've tried to spice it up by interjecting stories that add light and give you breaks along the way.

After our mindset shift, the first step is to align around what the problem is in the first place. Let's go.

CHAPTER EIGHT

- To succeed at change, we must pull our people through the change, not push.
- "Push" is about pushing our ideas onto people, telling them to change.
- "Pull" is about inspiring people to follow us, building infectiousness to what we're doing, engaging people's emotions and touching people's feelings.
- "Pull" is more likely to help people feel ownership of the change; it can become their idea.
- A pull mindset leads us to model the change and let our people take it from there rather than micromanaging how our direction gets executed.
- This can be hard for us because society believes the boss is the person who tells people what to do; we have to reorient and instead inspire people to do what's needed.

nine

We Align on the Problem

We find ourselves again at the company that had the fire drill that interrupted their crucial meeting on the need for change. With a combination of new data (temporarily better numbers) and other stuff ("Gotta minute?" "Can you look at this data?" etc.) they had allowed inertia to get in the way of their needed change.

In the months after this breakthrough/breakdown scenario, things only got worse for their business; those temporarily good numbers were just that: temporary. The board started pressuring the CEO; there could be no turning back. They brought in an outside consultant, Martha, to work with them. Although this was not the jerk we met in the Introduction, Martha held the same beliefs, and after some time, she helped them understand that it was, in fact, they themselves who needed to model the change—and to approach things from a mindset of pulling—if the change effort was going to be successful. They now had their heads around it.

Today they're at an off-site trying to think of ways to model the change, but the consultant keeps them focused on one thing at a time.

Consultant: Guys, I know we all want to think of ways to model the change. But sometimes we have to go slow to go fast. Let's start by answering this question: What's the problem forcing the change?

CFO: Well, Martha, we've done a lot of analysis on this. We all know what the problem is. We've done PowerPoint after PowerPoint on it.

COO: Yeah, seriously, Martha. I thought my team already sent you all the analysis on this. Did they not?

Consultant: I got it and read it, and it's good to know so much prechange analysis has already been done. It's just that I've worked with teams who are all over the map on what they say the problem is. So let's do an exercise. This'll be easy. On the piece of paper in front of you, I want each of you to describe in five words or less the problem as you see it.

At the top of each piece of paper, there's a statement. It

reads: "At the end of the day, the problem comes down to..." They finish, and Martha picks up the pieces of paper and starts reading them.

Consultant: OK, let's see what we have here. "A market share issue." "Inefficiency." "The IT platform." "Market share." "Technology." "Competitive product delivery." "Supply chain." "We are losing market share." "Operations issues."

People are looking around the room, confused, as she reads the list.

Consultant: So, does anyone want to apologize for the eye-rolling pushback I got when I asked all of you what the problem is?

CONSISTENTLY INCONSISTENT

This is typical. In fact, it's almost universal. We all assume everyone sees things the way we do. We're the normal ones, remember? Even though we've been through countless meetings and discussions together to get our heads around a problem, when it comes to explaining things in our own words, we often say things differently—even quite differently—depending on where we're coming from.

If we're leading sales and dealing with market share issues, we may point to product delivery—our biggest pain point stopping us from keeping up with competitors. If we're on the leadership team in operations, we may see it as an IT problem because that's our pain point. If we manage people in IT, we may call it a market share problem that we have to fix with technology. We're all dealing with it differently, and so we say different things.

And there's another reason people focus on one area of the problem while others focus elsewhere: we all want to talk to our own people about the problem from a standpoint that they'll understand best. Everyone in sales knows it's a market share issue already; their leadership communicates what's causing the market share issue: product delivery. People in IT know it's a tech problem; their leadership explains that the tech problem is causing market share erosion.

To the CEO and his team, this all makes logical sense, and it's easy to see how it all ties together. But to the IT employee (who hears that it's a market share problem) comparing notes with her husband who's in sales (and who's heard it's a product delivery problem), it's inconsistent. We can hear them talking about us: "Those idiots can't even be straight with us about what the hell the problem is."

It's not that our people aren't smart enough to connect the dots if we give them the dots; it's that we don't realize they're getting unconnectable dots to begin with. This is a "we" problem.

And—a reminder—our people have cognitive dissonance about the change we're putting them through. They want to go into the fetal position. They'll be as confused as they can be so—they hope—they can avoid the change presented to them (even if it's their subconscious driving the hope).

The consultant is right. Even if we blindly disbelieve it's happening in our specific case, we can easily dissect and communicate the problem inconsistently. It's noise. And there can't be any noise—not an inch of space—between us on this.

NOISE IS NOT GOOD

I should know. I had a part in one of the noisiest incidents ever. I'm not sure any other corporate-management-incongruence-leading-to-noise event has ever led to a national emergency, as this one did.

During my early career work on labor relations issues in both the railroad and airline industries, I helped a number of organizations through negotiations and even strikes. One company I was heavily engaged with reached a tentative agreement with one of its unions, and it seemed certain the rank-and-file employees would vote to confirm the contract. We knew that some individual members were not happy with the changes in the contract, but we assumed they were suffering from the natural cognitive dissonance—the "say it ain't so" feeling—we all have when change is in the offing.

All seemed to be going well until a member of senior management was in the field one day after the agreement was reached but before the vote. He struck up a conversation with some members of this work group, and they asked the executive about something their union was telling them. They said the union had explained in a certain way why management was asking for a certain change. The way they explained this either came from a game of telephone, or it was a trap being set.

Either way, the executive—a stickler for detail—said that a certain aspect of the union's explanation was wrong. The workers asked if the executive would put this in writing. He agreed to. Without notifying others in the organization, he followed through with a note.

Turned out, these workers were part of a group stridently opposed to the tentative contract, and they made sure this note—which unfortunately confused the issue—went viral. There was now space between managers. The union leadership lost support for the agreement, and more than 60 percent of the employees voted against the contract. What had seemed like a slam dunk became hostility. The parties very publicly girded for a strike on a very busy holiday weekend, with 24/7 coverage on cable news.

At least in part because of this noise among management at this company, the President of the United States had to intervene and declare a presidential emergency at the eleventh hour, stopping the strike. (Under the Railway Labor Act, governing only railroads and airlines, a president has the power to do this if he or she deems general commerce will be significantly disrupted.)

Noise is not good. There can't be space between managers on any of this, but especially not on the why.

FINDING CONSONANCE

Back to our executive off-site. I'll rewind things just a little bit: the consultant is reading what the executives each said the problem was, and this is revealing that they are not as united as they thought they were.

Consultant: OK, let's see what we have here. "A market share issue." "Inefficiency." "The IT platform." "Market share." "Technology." "Competitive product delivery." "Supply chain." "We are losing market share." "Operations issues."

People are looking around the room, confused, as she reads the list.

Consultant: So, does anyone want to apologize for the eye-rolling pushback I got when I asked all of you what the problem is?

Communications Leader: I can see how this could happen. See, the thing is, each of those explanations is right. Everyone's hitting on something that's true. We're losing market share because our antiquated technology platform is at its limits, so the technology constraints in supply chain are slowing our operations, and therefore, we're slow in delivering product to the customer.

Consultant: Yes, but to our people's ears, it sounds like we're saying different things. And they're putting the pieces together and calling bullshit on us. The good news is, I believe we can find a consonant common theme that ties it all together. What do we think that common thread is? Anyone want to take a crack?

COO: Well, we have an operational problem that's slowing down the supply chain, and that's slowing down time to customer.

Consultant: Uh-huh. It's an operations problem for sure, but what's the bottom line? What can everyone point to from every angle? Who's the most important stakeholder that we all have? We have one truth from which the others flow.

CIO: I think it comes down to the customer. Jim, like you tell us all the time, it should always come down to the customer.

CEO: That's right. We aren't delivering on time for the customer. If we fix that one outcome, we'll win. Our products are already better than the competition, and our product pipeline is very strong. I think what Martha is saying is that our one thing is delivering product to the customer faster.

Consultant: Right. So it's not all noise. There *is* a harmonious thread that runs through this. It's delivery time to the customer. In this case, to keep from confusing people, everyone must always explain this as *the* problem before explaining the closer-to-home problem that causes this ultimate problem or the closer-to-home problems that result from it. And instead of speaking about it as a problem, like, "We aren't delivering our product to our customers fast enough," we should say it in the affirmative. We should talk about a solution, like, "We have to deliver our product faster to our customers." Why don't you each try saying it?

Martha, the consultant, requires each participant to say it aloud: "We have to deliver our products faster to our customers."

Even the Sales Leader says it almost exactly like the others: "As you know, we have to deliver our products faster to our customers."

Consultant: That's great. As someone once said, "A problem well stated is a problem half solved."

HARMONY

This is a giant achievement. As noted, presidents have had to declare national emergencies because perfectly competent management teams *thought* they were in alignment but allowed space to get between them. We need to realize this can happen to us. We can't consider what the changes will be and how we'll communicate them until we have complete agreement on what the challenge is and how we'll explain the components making up this why.

Sometimes, consensus and alignment are easily reached among the team; other times, it requires us to "disagree and commit," as mentioned in Chapter 4. Either way, we must eliminate the ugly noise and communicate the why in a consonant way. But how?

One of the ugliest sounds in the world (according to my ears) is the sound of symphony musicians testing their instruments just before a concert. Each is trying to ensure their instrument is ready, but they're not doing it in any consonant way. Individually, they may be doing something very important. Collectively, they're making ugly noise.

This is what differing messages can sound like to the untrained ears of the employees who already have cognitive dissonance about a big change coming their way. Remember, they're often looking for the slightest inconsistency—even if they're doing it subconsciously—to give themselves hope they can avoid the change.

So how do we cater to the ears of individual employee groups while also having an explanation that holds together for all employees? The answer lies a few moments after we hear the ugly collective noise from the individual symphony musicians. After a few notes, we get our answer: harmony.

With harmony, we get many different sounds, or parts, being played at once. The genius is in the beautiful consonance of the pitches and synchronous rhythm (played by the entire group). These different pitches—played in synchrony—make a combined sound that's more powerful and gracious to the ear than if every member of the symphony played the exact same notes throughout the piece of music.

Harmony is how we attack the challenge of having different angles to explain the ultimate issue that's requiring the change.

In the symphony, just before the maestro comes out, the concert master (the lead violinist) asks the lead oboist to play an A for the strings section; they tune to A. Then the lead oboist plays the same A for the wind and brass sections, and they all tune to A. So they're now tuned to the same wavelength. This is the equivalent of the meeting we just observed...the aha that they needed to get on the same page with the why.

For this example, the orchestra is about to play Beethoven's Fifth Symphony. (If you don't know it offhand, you're sure to recognize it when you go out and listen to it. And if you're not able to listen to it right now, just know that it's a musical piece that starts with four simple notes played strongly, and throughout the rest of the piece it features these notes prominently time and again.)

In our work, we start by reaching consensus on how we explain the overall problem. This is the theme of the musical piece. In Beethoven's Fifth, the theme is the first four notes of the piece. We hear the theme time and again throughout the piece. Even when we depart from the theme, we come back to it.

For our purposes, we'll play the theme motif—the first four notes—in unison. When we play it, we'll always play the theme by playing the same exact notes as each other. No member of our symphony will depart. We don't deviate when we come back to communicating the theme, either. The theme—the core why—is the theme.

In a practical sense, for us, when we say, "We have to deliver our products faster to our customers," we have no reason to say it differently. Even our sales leader says it the same way, adding the line "As you know" before the statement to keep his team from thinking he's dense for stating what's obvious to them.

Sections of the Orchestra

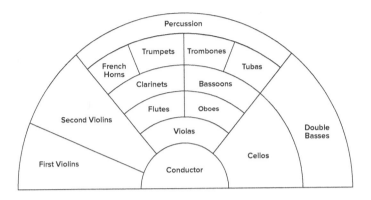

Our Organization in Harmony

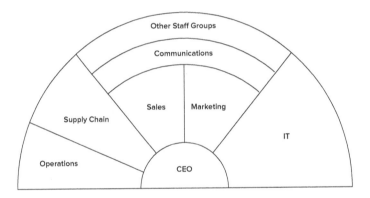

We're in unison. And we keep coming back to the theme time and again. No one in our organization can escape the theme. We never tire of the theme; it's our North Star. Just as with GEICO and its "fifteen minutes" bit, we come up with clever ways to include it in as many places as possible. It's simple. It's recognizable. Everyone can understand it and explain it. It drips from the walls.

And just like at GEICO, we know that repetition—while it bores our own ears, while we think everyone else is bored with it—we know that our audience is not hearing it anywhere nearly as often as we're saying it, so we remain disciplined.

Think of Houston and the moon shot in the 1960s. In that era, if you asked any person involved in that effort what he or she did for a living—whether they were a statistician or a janitor—they would say, "I'm helping to put a man on the moon and return him safely." Everyone knew the line and what it meant.

What we're doing has to be as important to us as it was to Houston. It's important to our own livelihoods, to our people, and to our customers: "We have to deliver our products faster to our customers."

When we go beyond just stating the theme, we work in harmony. There are times when this harmony is about playing different notes, but any employee—upon hearing it—would recognize it or at least understand it if it's heard being played by another instrument.

At other times, we play a variation—with purpose—that strays from the theme. We may play in the round or we may even go off temporarily on our own motif—our own set of notes.

The theme is: "We have to deliver our products faster to our customers." A variation might be: "We must improve our IT platform and our own processes because (back to the theme) we have to deliver our products faster to our customers." Another statement could be: "We need to improve our supply chain and take advantage of forthcoming tech improvements because (theme) we have to deliver our products faster to our customers."

This is crucial. There can be no distance between leaders when stating the theme, and we have to constantly come back to the same theme in the same way, or our people will find a way to be confused.

STAYING IN TUNE

A note of caution: this is the symphony; it's not jazz. As much as I love jazz and the constant innovation it provides the artist and the listener, when working on a change initiative, we have to leave the innovation and serious riffing out of our communications. Unless we're hoping to confuse our people, we don't come up with wildly different riffs.

Another note of caution: watch out for the musician who decides to have their own ideas for how to explain things—using completely different pieces of music. I've seen people on executive teams act like they're in harmony with the others on these things, only to rethink it all by themselves and come up with a completely different way to explain things.

At a startup business I was a part of—a business that brought several units together—we started out by spending a lot of time as an extended leadership team collectively developing a mission, values, and goals. A month later, one executive and her team went off and developed their own mission, values, and goals. I remember having two thoughts: (1) "What a difficult executive," and (2) "Is our mission inclusive enough? Did she do this because we didn't include her voice enough in the decision-making process?" We should always look at it as a potential "we" problem.

CLOSING NOTE

Bottom line: we'll always be susceptible to being discordant in how we think and what we say when explaining what's at the heart of the need for change. We have to respect that this can happen—even to little old us. We can't be noisy, so we have to do the hard work of making sure that we're in unison on the core reason and that we're in harmony when explaining the aspects that apply to our teams.

And as we'll see in Chapter 10, we can ensure the music is great music only if we listen before composing it.

CHAPTER NINE

- Every member of leadership—as low down as we can go—must know and give the same explanation for why the change is necessary.
- Any distance between explanations of this why can crush a change initiative. Executives need to explain the same why every time. Yet distance between executives on this is almost universal unless they work to get it right.
- Change will impact groups differently, so leaders need room to explain the specifics to their individual work groups. But it can't come at the cost of improvising on the overall reason for change.
- We speak in unison when addressing the why for the change.
- We speak in harmony when addressing things from our work groups' angle, and we return back to the original why in unison as often as possible.

TEN

We Listen

As our executive team continues its work at the off-site meeting, they learn once more that launching this change effort—if they want it to be successful and enduring—isn't going to be as easy or as quick as they thought.

Consultant: I know you guys are eager to make progress on the meat of the issue—to decide what needs to be cut and how to model the change—but you haven't even told your people you're thinking of making changes, and you haven't asked them for input. You think you'll succeed if you foist the change on them? You guys need to spend time with your team gathering ideas for the types of changes to make.

CEO: You mean to tell me we flew to this off-site to come up with "We have to deliver our product faster to our customers," and it's time to go home?

Consultant: Well, no, we'll spend the afternoon planning

how we'll solicit ideas. Also, tomorrow, we'll conduct some active listening and meeting management training. You guys seem to keep scoring low in those areas, and you need good listening and meeting management skills to bring good ideas out of your people.

PULL FOR CONSENSUS

As we did when arriving at an explanation for the problem, we need to just as clearly reach consensus on what changes we'll pull for in the organization. And everyone on the team must have—and believe they've had—a part in the process. This goes beyond the team at the off-site.

Remember, we're pulling, not pushing. We need people's involvement in this process. As Dan Gilbert, founder of Quicken Loans, said, "Please give me all your feedback immediately." And he succeeded, remember?

But according to Gartner, more than 80 percent of the organizations they studied use a top-down approach to their change programs: the senior leadership team makes the strategic decisions with little or no input from others, they develop the plans for implementation, and they announce it through traditional communications to get buy-in.

This may seem faster for them, and it may have worked in the days of blue memos when organizations were hierarchical. But today's change-failure rate tells us the payoff is abysmal. We're better off going slow to go fast. This is for at least four reasons.

First, we want our people pulling with us, not taking incoming fire from us. If they're taking incoming fire, they're likely to be confused and less engaged. If we engage them in the planning, the implementation will be much less rough. The old 90 percent preparation and 10 percent perspiration thought applies here: we're engaging them in the preparation, so there's less perspiration in the execution.

Second, today's organizations are no longer top-down beasts. They're flatter, groups are much more interconnected and interdependent, and employees today have access to more information.

Third, leaders don't really know what's going on. We need to admit we don't know all of the workflow interdependencies of our much more complex organizations. So our ideas—especially for implementation—are much more likely to be naïve. Employees, on the other hand, can figure out how to implement the change more effectively, and they're much more likely to *want* to pull the change forward if they've been involved in the planning process.

Fourth, we should never underestimate the simple power of listening. Not only might it yield better ideas, but it can lead to very unexpected, helpful behavior. On two occasions when I was leading a change effort on my own team, and I explained the challenge and listened, then listened some more, then continued listening, I had people each time in the primes of their careers come to me and tell me they thought their positions should be eliminated. I was not expecting this at all. People will do very unconventional things if they're listened to...if they feel heard.

LISTENING FORMALIZED

We can't bring in every employee to analyze the market problem, the why. But it certainly makes sense to bring in leaders at different levels of the organization and get their insight on the problem. We also want their ideas for planning the change. McKinsey & Company reports that successful organizations were four times as likely to have brought in fifty or more people to plan their change versus the unsuccessful organizations they studied.

It's as much about getting these leaders' thoughts (we may gain insight we hadn't foreseen) as it is about bringing them in—getting their support so that when they later have to talk with employees about the change and the why behind it, they feel comfortable doing it. These leaders may not even be the senior-most, next-level employees; they could simply be well-respected, change-oriented leaders from a range of levels and areas of the organization.

Some will worry about the rumor mill that might result from bringing in these leaders. ("Word will get out!") The rumor mill can be a pain, it can upset productivity in the here and now, but in our new world of ubiquitous information, we need to recognize that the days of controlling the message at every stage are over. Also, the huffing and puffing of senior people spending all their time hiding things and then worrying that something has gotten out—not only is this an unproductive use of their time, but it also creates an us-versus-them feeling that erodes the trust we'll need for execution. Remember, unlike fine wine, bad news does not get better with age, so the idea that we should try to hold on to it until we have all the answers to push onto people— that's not what we're going for.

What's most important—what will matter most a year or two from now, long after we've announced it—is that the outcome we decided upon was right and fair and not naive, that we authentically searched for the right way to bring forth the best change possible. Bringing in others for their ideas is very important to this. (Of course, some information, such as material nonpublic information about a public company, can't be easily revealed selectively.)

WHERE TO ERR

As to whether all of the to-be-affected employees should help determine what the change is, the success statistics tell us we should definitely err on the side of inclusion. According to Gartner, when organizations use what it calls an "open source" approach to change planning (formalized listening), employees throughout the organization are much more likely to understand the change going forward.

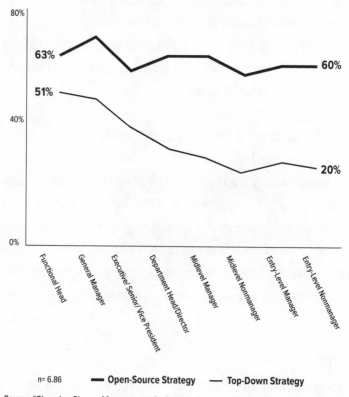

Top-Down Change Strategies Reduce Understanding of Change in the Workforce

Percentage of Respondents Understanding Change by Seniority

n= 6.86 ━━ **Open-Source Strategy** ── **Top-Down Strategy**

Source: "Changing Change Management: An Open-Source Approach," Gartner, 2019

Including more people—while potentially messy—may also bring us rich ideas that we couldn't possibly imagine. (We've hired smart, sophisticated people—some of them smarter than us.) Also, don't forget that we want to pull them through the change as much as possible and do less pushing change on them, so having them involved in some way is desirable. Finally, we have a much greater chance of converting those on the sidelines (the "but I'm trying," the "I need more information," and even the "politically correct" people) if we make the change clearer and more real by involving them.

I've seen (and been a part of) organizations that spent a whole lot of time and energy getting insight from people at every level for various initiatives—in addition to my own eye-opening listening efforts with my own teams, where people volunteered to leave.

During my time at American Airlines, Boston Consulting Group led us through a change assessment in the mid-1990s for management cost reductions called "activity value analysis." Everyone in management participated by evaluating every activity we performed, and we and our internal clients placed values on these activities. We made cuts based on these values.

When developing our purpose at GE Aviation, we pulsed more than ten thousand employees during group sessions, asking them what each of them thought the division's purpose was. From the reams of insight, our partners at the Purpose Institute, led by Roy Spence, found three threads that summed it up well: "We invent the future of flight, lift people up, and bring them home safely." The purpose is still the heart of the division's thinking a decade later.

IBM has done some terrific work here for almost two decades with their Jams—two-day online idea-generating opportunities for every employee. Their ValuesJam allowed people to comment on proposed changes to IBM's principles. Many other organizations have followed suit with these types of online activities.

And like my own small-scale listening experiences with my teams, listening efforts at scale can be fruitful. At Pixar, in search of a 10 percent reduction in unit costs for each movie (from 22,000-person weeks to 18,500-person weeks), the leadership team created what was called "Notes Day." They shut down completely for a day. Beforehand, every member of the team was encouraged to offer ideas for cost savings, then they crowdsourced to determine the main topics of discussion. Employees owned the day and its direction by their votes, which dictated how many sessions there would be on how many given topics.

The number one requested topic, and the most popular session: How do we make a movie with 12,000-person weeks?

They had to arrange seven separate sessions to include everyone who wanted to offer ideas on this topic. They immediately implemented several ideas, moved quickly to implement several more, and they continued working on still more over time.

People at Pixar had to know that if unit costs were cut from 22,000-person weeks to 12,000-person weeks, a lot of jobs might go missing. But they were *in*. They were invigorated because their company wanted to hear their ideas, and so they wanted to have a say in the future of *their* company. They *wanted* to change.

Bottom line: we need to err on the side of transparency whenever we can. The days of controlling the message are over...gone...done. We needn't spend all our time worrying about secrets—they won't matter a year from now. What *will* matter are our actions—whether we were fair in the end and open along the way.

And we should err on the side of involvement as much as we can. A union president I knew once said to the management executives he negotiated with, "When you buy a pair of hands, you get the brain for free." And as Pixar's and my own experience shows, when you excite the brains of your people, when you help them understand that their ideas are critical to your change, and you listen sincerely, all kinds of unexpectedly helpful things can happen.

WHILE WE WERE AWAY

Let's go back to the executive team at its next off-site three months later.

Consultant: First, congratulations on how well you all embraced the why that we have for the change and how you garnered so much good input from your teams. You listened. Your people are in a different place than they would have been if you had simply foisted some change on them. They're nervous, no doubt, but they don't feel the helplessness they would be feeling if you hadn't gone to them openly and shared the challenge and told them what you're up to.

COO: Martha, I just want to let you know that I was pissed off when you told us we needed to take that active listening class. In fact, I don't think anyone could have been angrier about it. I was insulted. But I begrudgingly took the course. And as a result of that class, I spent four days on the floor at our Poughkeepsie site. One night, I spent an overnight in the FedEx room. I just helped scan out packages. They knew who I was, so they were fascinated that I would spend time scanning out packages. But what I learned was wicked helpful. I just listened to the people all around me. Actually, they didn't have to say anything; they just trained me on their systems. Man, their work lives are even crazier than I imagined. We've totally set them up for failure. So thanks for knocking my head around and making me take that course. I've been sharing what I learned with the whole team, and I think we're even more ready to make the right changes than we would have been before.

Consultant: That's good to hear...glad it was helpful. Now, with all the insight you gained, let's focus on the changes. I think everyone knows the problem is that we have to deliver our products faster to our customers. So what changes are needed to make that happen?

What follows is a series of presentations from IT, Operations, HR and Finance that reflect the ideas of people throughout the organization. The CIO talks about how her team is going to overhaul the tech platform, including a very different tech stack. The COO assures everyone that Operations and Supply Chain believe IT's work is attacking the right problems, and he talks about how his groups will ready themselves for the changes in their systems and processes. The HR leader talks about staffing needs in IT, Operations, and Supply Chain as a result of all of these changes. Other members of the team chime in with ideas they've heard from their own teams. The CFO talks about how much all of this will cost.

CEO: So we know it's going to cost twenty percent of annual revenue up front just to make these changes, and then it's going to cost ten percent per year ongoing. We have to fund this somehow, and I've heard many of your opinions on this.

Consultant: Just as important, when we talk about how we fund all of this—about what the changes are—we also need to think ahead to how we'll model the change, how we show we're supporting it. If we mandate change and can find no way to model what we decide upon, it'll just be mandated change. And like we discussed before, change by decree—alone—is change on the cheap. It doesn't stick. We can have all the logic in the world behind the changes, but to change behavior we need to change hearts, not just minds. That means we need to have our own hearts in this, or we'll be wasting a lot of time and money on a change that won't last.

CEO: Well, I have to tell you, I don't think anyone's heart is going to be into what we have to do. If you like cutting costs, meaning probably cutting jobs, you have no heart.

Consultant: I understand.

CEO: So let's talk about this.

Consultant: It's really important that we start with the organization's values. If we just start stating the need for change and how we all need to change, there's no change context that's aligned with our values that ties it all together. You're about to embark on the change; don't just cut a bunch of jobs and programs. Do it in a context that helps others have the same mindset—especially the people who you want to remain here. Do it in a context that will endure. Obviously, it also needs to tie in to the theme of the problem. Plus, it's what informs how we'll model the change. Are we ready for another exercise?

The consultant gets up to the white board, and the team starts brainstorming about the context for the change. We see words like "nimble," "modernize," "cost-efficient," "invest," "faster." They look at their core values, which include, "We win only by serving our customers well," and "We run a tight ship." They synthesize this into principles of customers and cost efficiency for the change context. And they arrive at a context entitled "Giving it up for the customer."

CEO: So that's it. We have to deliver our products faster to our customers. That's forcing some investment. So we have to reduce costs to afford this investment. "We're giving it up for the customer." See, I included the core theme from the last off-site, "deliver our products faster to our customers," *and* the context. See how I did that?

Everyone nods approvingly at their proud CEO!

CONTEXT IS KEY

As we'll see when we talk about determining how to model the change, change context is key. This is another thing the successful change efforts we've studied had in common, even if there wasn't always a stated change context per se, it was there to be found in each case.

- Dan Gilbert—when he pulled his people to join the internet—his change context might well have been "Let's not miss out on our future."
- Michelle Peluso at Travelocity—when she modeled the change by allowing customers to take the $1 fare to Fiji—the change context was "customer championship," which had become an implicit value. We had spoken about customer championship to the team with a presentation titled "Are You a Champion?" When she responded to the Fiji Airways pricing mishap the way she did, she modeled customer championship brilliantly.
- When he exclusively took the subway—and used his example to encourage his key staff members to take the subway regularly—William Bratton was doing it in a change context we might call "We're all riders." After experiencing it himself, he figured if he could get his people to see, smell, feel and touch what riders were experiencing each day, their empathy would give them a sense of urgency to make things better.
- When he started holding his one-on-one meetings in the new social space, the furniture manufacturing executive was acting on a change context that we might call "Let's do like our customers and get better at collaborating."

The term "change context" may be a new one, but now that we've identified this concept, we can proactively develop and use a change context in our own change efforts so everyone can take ownership of it.

DETERMINING THE CHANGES

Back at the off-site, the consultant is getting the team to determine the changes.

Using previously developed data and analysis, plus inputs from their own teams, various leaders offer suggestions for how their teams can be nimbler and more cost efficient. (Now that they have the context, it informs their thinking.) Then they get into specific areas of the business and how they'll change. The CIO talks about moving to agile development. The CFO and HR Leader talk about outsourcing some less important tasks. The Operations Leader talks about what he and his team will need to do to ready the supply chain and other areas for more efficient input and throughput once the technology comes online. Everyone joins in when the HR Leader talks about adjusting resources (additions and subtractions); it's decided that the big hits will come in staff jobs—centralizing staff functions that are currently decentralized—as well as some other areas such as marketing (brand, pricing), cutting consulting budgets, tightening contingency budgets, and smaller cuts throughout other organizations. IT and Operations will gain resources.

Together, the team determines what success will look like and how they'll know when they've reached it. All of the leaders talk about how they'll remove some less important work and take on more of the day-to-day work...enough to help cover some of the missing people but without completely killing their time to think.

Developing a Change Context and Informing How We Model the Change

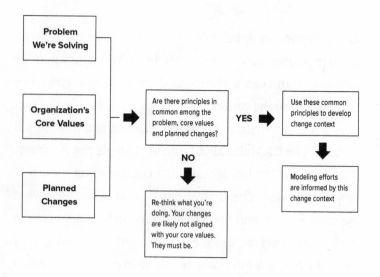

Example We've Studied

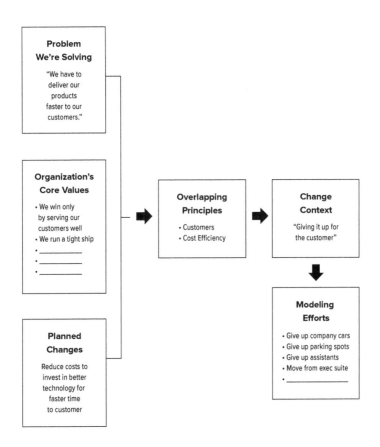

IT'S NOT EASY

This isn't easy work because it involves people's lives and their careers, but it's a major victory for the success of the overall organization and its future, which is important for the lives and careers of the many, many people who will remain once the change is in place. But, as we'll see in the next chapter, the hearts and minds of the teams who have to change—those who have to centralize where they were decentralized, move to agile development, retool the supply chain and other areas, and thin out in almost every area of the organization—these people who will have to transform their organizations, as well as the people working for them, and the people working for them—their hearts and minds are still very much up for grabs.

CHAPTER TEN

- Once we agree on the reason for the change and how we'll say it and tell our own organization's story, we must involve our people in the change if we can.
- Organizations that include their people in change planning are much more likely to be successful than those that had top-down change management.
- Listening is critical in change. Although it can be messy, organizations that involve and listen to their people can get surprisingly positive results.
- We must also develop a change context that ties into our reason for the change, incorporates our values, and informs how we model the change appropriately. This process ensures our change is not out of line with our values.
- What's most important—what will matter most a year from now, long after we've announced the change—is that the outcome was right and fair and not naive, and that we authentically searched for the right way to bring forth the best change possible.

ELEVEN

We Model the Change

So we've agreed on a harmonic way to explain the why... the reason we need to change our organization: "We have to deliver our products faster to our customers." This is our theme.

We've listened to our people to determine the how...the method we'll use to change our organization. We'll lower costs to invest in things that will help us deliver our products faster to our customers.

And this is aligned with the change context we developed: "giving it up for the customer." This context ties into our values, our change theme, and how we'll model the change.

It's time to use this change context to determine how we model the change.

FINDING THE BOLD ACTIONS

Another quick visit to our off-site.

CEO: So how do we fulfill the change context? Anyone want to think of ways we model "giving it up for the customer"?

HR Leader: This can't be about giving up things for Lent. It has to be stuff we'll give up permanently.

Communications Leader: Yeah. It has to be pretty bold, visible action that makes a statement. People will see through it if we aren't authentic about what we're giving up, or if it's not on par with the kind of changes they're having to make.

CIO: I've already decided on one thing for my own change. I'm going to help train teams in agile development; better to get everyone engaged and understanding how important this change is—even if I'm awfully busy with everyday stuff—than to have to do a change program all over again because the initial change failed. Failure would potentially double my everyday stuff later.

CEO: Wow, Jean, that's great. That's really modeling change.

CFO: It really is. I have another idea. You know, we're the only people here who still have our own assistants. I can keep my own schedule, make my own coffee and copies. I don't have that many needs.

COO: Well, I hate that idea, but your point is true. As much as I really rely on Sam, I can't justify having that much support. I'm willing to make that change too.

HR Leader: I think we can share assistants, maybe one for three? That's the standard for other leaders.

CEO: OK. This is going to hurt for all of us, but I can't see how we can justify having company cars and dedicated parking spaces when we're asking our people to accept cuts. Company cars and parking spaces for executives—that's actually pretty old-school stuff. I can't believe we haven't gotten rid of these things already.

Sales Leader: Some of my salespeople will still need company cars, but I guess I can give up mine. It hurts, though.

CEO: I'll let you buy your current company cars at a good price if that makes you any happier.

COO: We can move out of the executive floor and make space for some of the new IT and Operations people, and we can move into smaller offices either together or separately.

Communications Leader: If we move in with our people, we might not be as close as an executive team, but we would be closer to our people, and that might give us better insight into what's actually happening. There's something to be said for a leadership team that has its ear to the ground.

They continue and come up with a few smaller changes.

FIRST, DO NO HARM

The team we've been observing has had to make some tough personal and professional sacrifices to make it clear they're sharing in the pain. But all modeling isn't as drastic as what this team is doing. Taking the subway each day. Showing people what customer championship looks like. Holding all our meetings in a new open space. Asking people to come with us on a journey to a thing called the internet. It can come in many shapes and sizes, depending on the change we're going for and many other factors.

Some may wonder, "Well, how little can I change my ways and still model change?" Shame on you for asking that, but it's true that we don't have to metamorphose from caterpillar to butterfly in order to see some changes through. The better question may be, "What changes do I need to make so the change gets full support?"

Sometimes it's a matter of supporting others' change initiatives.

In any organization, there are almost always change

agents—people who are naturally inclined to see things differently and help bring about a change. They can be at any level and hold any number of jobs. I've seen administrative assistants act as change agents; no one should underestimate the passion people have when they believe the organization needs change, and they feel they can help make that change happen or even lead it.

Also, don't underestimate the frustration perfectly passionate people will feel when we—anyone above them, from frontline manager to CEO—will not support the change they're trying to usher in, especially if we've asked for it. It's easy for great people to feel helpless and hopeless when they can't get the support they need for something they're passionate about.

And it's easy to show we don't support the change. We can roll our eyes about some aspect of the change. Innocently tease a change agent in a meeting about the change. Call the change a funny term. It's easy to kill change.

Deeper still, we'll make it almost impossible for these change agents if we're the kind of leader who generally pooh-poohs change in the off-season. "That thing called the Twitter or whatever," was a statement I once heard a leader say as he smiled and rolled his eyes. He was giving all his people license to stay away from it. He wasn't challenging them to find out what Twitter—and other similar capabilities—were about and how they could be used to create competitive advantage.

So, yes, we can do some lighter work by supporting a change, but first, do no harm. We don't position ourselves well if we're generally dismissive of new things, and our people will see right through us if we suddenly morph from pooh-pooher in chief to Mr. Change.

DO IT EVERY DAY

In 2007—just as sites like Facebook and Myspace were taking hold—my own organization, the travel technology company Sabre, decided to join the mix and develop an internal social networking capability for employees.

The company was globalizing, going from 85 percent US-based employees to only 40 percent US-based employees in five years. Colleagues weren't seated down the hall anymore; we couldn't get to know them as well, even if we worked with them regularly across time zones and phone calls. Our CEO, Sam Gilliland, recognized that this was monumental change, and he asked us to help him with it to find ways to narrow the chasm.

With my own proclivity for championing change, I had started an initiative to make it possible for employees to post photographs on the intranet and even answer a few questions about their areas of expertise and even their personal lives. The idea: if I have a meeting with Jane Doe in Montevideo in a few minutes, let me find out more about who I'm talking with.

John Samuel, a colleague of mine, came to me because he had heard I was trying to make the intranet a better source for collaboration. John, too, had always been on the leading edge of change, ever since we worked together at another company in the 1990s when he was introducing websites, business software, and other advanced tools of the day.

In this case, he had a technology platform left over from a failed community site, and he wanted to see if there was another use for it. In the previous iteration of the software, his leisure travel agent clients—who now worked from home—were no longer in a storefront with two or three other agents who collectively knew every part of the world. They now needed to connect somehow with other at-home travel agents to learn and share advice about unfamiliar locales.

John's team had built a community platform that could do this. Each travel agent would fill out a profile, and when a travel agent inquired about a topic on the platform, this intelligent system would email the handful of travel agents who were most likely to know the topic.

John shared this with me, and it took no time for me to

realize we could do a lot more to promote collaboration and get-to-know-ness throughout the organization. We could do more than just putting photos and info about our kids on the intranet. This capability was ripe for our internal needs. We needed to build it and champion it.

What resulted was a great tool that allowed for global collaboration. "Does anyone know William Sipford at Millennium Hotels?" could be answered by people from several lines of business who worked with that chain. "I have Italian clients coming to town. Does anyone speak Italian at headquarters?" was, in fact, answered by Fabio, who sat three cubicle rows down from the inquirer. We called this tool SabreTown.

The problem at first was—as with the collaboration space at the furniture manufacturer—only the "What have we been waiting fors?" used it. Everyone else sat on the sidelines. To drive usage, we even encouraged people to use it for personal questions, but most people complied by filling out a profile and going back to work. This was, after all, 2007; social networking was still foreign to most people, and they also likely asked, "Would my bosses really allow me to hang out on a social networking website at work? They'll know I'm doing it."

Then an employee in London was wondering how she could count laps in the pool as she trained for a swim race. She asked the question of the SabreTown community. As it happened, our CEO Sam Gilliland was a swimmer, and the system emailed the question to him, among others. He was the first to answer it, giving his technique for remembering what lap he was on.

Word spread, and usage of SabreTown took off. Within a couple of months, we had more than 80 percent adoption. Most of it was for personal use at first, but by the end of 2008, 60 percent was for business use. Sam had shown support for his change agents.

So it looks like all Sam had to do was answer one stinking question and he's suddenly a modeler of change. Not so fast. First of all, at last check, to this day Sam still doesn't do much social networking; it wasn't his thing then, and it isn't his thing now. But the tool made it easy by sending him an email to answer. Easy enough.

More important, if Sam had been the kind of CEO who rolled his eyes at change or laughed off any of the off-the-wall suggestions, his action with the London swimmer very well may have looked contrived. People are savvy; they know when they're being sold a bill of goods. Long gone are the days when a communications person could get her CEO to do something out of character and have people believe it. Out-of-synch actions won't sustain change.

Sam was the kind of leader who looked for and encouraged new ideas. His use of SabreTown wasn't out of character, even if he was by no means a social media maven.

SabreTown may have been far ahead of its time, but the idea of modeling behavior to show support is timeless. Sam Gilliland didn't have to change every habit of his workday, but he had to sincerely support SabreTown, and he had to be seen as—and authentically be—someone open to change.

Had he not modeled the behavior and not answered the question, no one might have noticed. But, then again, Sam and Sabre might have missed the collaboration, the cost savings, and the capabilities that SabreTown brought his enterprise for several years. He—and Sabre—would have missed out on the change he was going for as we continued to globalize.

Bottom line: depending on the change we're going for, we can indeed model the change we want just by showing support. But support for change can't be a one-time thing. We must love our change agents. No eye-rolling or cute comments when they walk into a meeting. They may be moonbeams, but they're *our* moonbeams, dammit, and they will likely be the people who first support us when we finally realize we need change throughout our organization.

It doesn't matter the size of the change—from transformational or a simple process change—we have to be supportive, or it will have a much harder time flying.

AND THEN...

One last visit to our executive team. Later that night at the bar, our executives are thinking back on the work they've done, and the results they've produced.

Sales Leader: So we're giving up our assistants, we're giving up our company cars and our parking spots, and we had to take active listening and meeting management training. Isn't this what that consultant we never hired called for? Remember who I'm talking about, that consultant who said she wouldn't work for us unless we did exactly this? We all thought she was a jerk, remember?

Strategy Leader: No, that person *was* a jerk. She didn't suggest any of this.

CFO: Seriously, what makes you think she suggested any of that? We came up with all of it.

CEO: Actually, this is exactly what she told us we would need to do—and more.

HR Leader: I think you're right. I guess we needed it to be our own idea. I guess that was her problem; she was going to push us...we needed to be pulled...or to pull ourselves toward the changes.

CEO: And it's OK if you don't remember. That meeting was before the active listening course that Martha put us through!

CHAPTER ELEVEN

- Once we have the reason for the change down pat, and we know the context for the change based on the reason plus our values, and once we know what the changes will be, it's time to determine how we model the change.
- We use the change context to inform how we'll model the change.
- We've seen examples for modeling change many times in this book; all of them had a change context, whether it was stated or not.
- If our change context is "giving it up for the customer" and we're cutting costs, this informs us that we need to give things up as well.
- Modeling change can come in many forms, including simply supporting a change happening lower in the organization. But our actions—our modeling—can look contrived if they aren't authentic, if our actions are uncharacteristic of what we usually do. That makes change management an everyday part of our jobs as leaders.

Conclusion

We All Have Choices

So we have choices. We can decide to put window dressing on cheap change efforts, or we can grow ourselves and do the hard work of ushering in real change. We can hope the change sticks, or we can ensure it will endure—by our own actions, by finding ways to model the change, by being the change. We can be the kind of leaders who pooh-pooh our change agents' ideas, or we can realize we'll need these change agents someday, and we can—as part of our natural, everyday personas—be the kinds of leaders who are open to ideas. Because, ultimately, we aren't trying to get people to change; we're trying to get people to *want* to change.

We've concluded that this is a "we" problem, not a "they" problem. "Theyak" is not a word, but it reminds us that we're "weak" when we think the solution starts with "they" (other leaders, middle management, frontline employees, etc.). We are the enemies of change, but we're redeemable:

- We can recognize that we (and our people) have anxiety about the uncertainty of change, brought on by psychological discomfort, and we can account for this every step of the change effort.
- We can take a new look at what traditional communications can and cannot do—especially in today's information landscape—and how critical our actions are in anything we want to communicate. Action speaks louder than words—we've heard this line, now we need to live it.
- We can be better managers of ourselves, not allowing inertia to get in the way of the hard work we must do as leaders, and by taking much-needed time out to re-create and think anew.
- We can recognize that change by decree—while it may feel like an easy win, while it forces immediate or near-term compliance, and while it may look good for board presentations—it's change on the cheap. It won't last, it won't make our organization competitive for the long term, and it's not aligned with our values. (Whatever our values may be, they don't include "comply, comply, comply.")
- We can keep our eyes on the big picture, not the weeds, and recognize that heart is central to successful SMART work. We want to drive behavior change here, so we

must win over our people's hearts if we have any chance of driving specific, measurable, achievable, relevant, and timely results. We can't be one-dimensional with change efforts—only focusing on the intellect, not focusing on the emotional levers we must pull to bring our people with us. And our change must be aligned with our values.

- We can recognize that different people will react differently to change efforts, so we need to manage them differently.

We know that successful leaders take the time to pull their people through change rather than pushing change on their teams. This way, their people take ownership because we're along on the change journey with them.

We now have insight into how to develop the why—explaining succinctly why we need to change, explaining it in synchrony with each other, and without assumption that we're on the same page. We know that when we create the how—the actual ways the organization needs to change—that we need to do it in a context that allows us as leaders to model that change. And we grappled with the many, many different ways leaders can model change—from the very bold to the very supportive.

All of this, I hope, pulls us to a place that—while humbling—makes us more ready to change as leaders, more ready to model the change so our work leads to lasting changes in our organizations. I hope it helps us make the right choices, helps us recognize that change starts with "we" (which includes "me"), not others. I hope it helps us become better leaders.

NOW IT'S YOUR TIME

So now that you've read this book and acted on it, your people are primed for change. And it's now time to execute your change effort, going beyond the dimension I've focused on—which is about developing an emotional way to get people to *want* to change. It's now time for the executional dimension (the SMART, the intellectual, the rational portion). This book doesn't tell you how to do the SMART work because many, many other books and change management consultants do. Instead, it focuses on heart, the input. Once we have the hearts enrolled—in the boat, paddling with us—our people are primed for change, and we can start attacking the change at hand.

Growing up on the Gulf Coast, I remember TV ads from a company called Western. I'm not sure what they did—it was something in the oil industry. They had a tagline that said, "If you don't have an oil well, get one. You'll love doing business with Western."

To you, I say, "If you don't know how to lead and to model

change, learn how by stepping out and trying it. You'll love the leader you become and the things you make happen."

If you ever have questions about what I've written here, feel free to contact me at al@alcomeaux.com.

I wish you good luck and great change.

Acknowledgments

Writing this book took me on a journey from the brain's amygdala to the symphony to the dot-com boom to the bowels of the New York subways in the 1990s to the early days of commercial computing to the highways of Texas to many other places, both real and metaphorical. This journey would not have been possible without the help of friends and strangers alike.

My wife, Katie, was ever supportive, offering ideas and insights, and our daughters were good sports through all the time Dad worked on—and was distracted by—his book. All of my siblings showed me loving excitement during my work on this book, as did my wife's family. Thanks for all the encouragement.

Dan Simon, who—several days after I first told him about this concept—called out of the blue to tell me he couldn't stop thinking about the idea, well, that was encourage-ment. Marsha Clark, Ginger Hardage, Josh Rovner, Robert Kallam, and my brother Andre Comeaux, all encouraged me to write this book once I described my idea. It takes encouragement to get the ball rolling. Thanks.

I received ideas and early editing support from many people, including Marsha Clark, Joanne Cleaver, Chris Chiames, Jonathan Walker, Scott Trahan, and my brother Andre. A panel of C-level beta readers helped me refine it further; thanks to Sam Gilliland, Kathy Boden Hol-land, Barry Vandevier, and Chris Moffett for their ideas and encouragement.

Thanks also to Mike Pacchione and Jayson Teagle for reviewing the manuscript and helping me think about how I could bring this book to life in other ways.

I couldn't have completed this book without the help of the team at Scribe Media and Lioncrest, including Tucker Max, Hal Clifford, Emily Gindlesparger, Ian Claudius, Cindy Curtis, Erica Hoffman, April Kelly, Will Tyler, Holly Gorman, Jessi Cimafonte, Michael Nagin, and Erin Tyler. My editor, Jenny Shipley, gave me great guidance in so many areas. Thanks also for the accountability that my cohort at Scribe expected of me.

Michael Waschevski and Kathryn Perry gave me great

insights into how the symphony and harmony work and don't work; any mistakes are mine (as they are throughout the book).

Content help came from Steve Clampett, Whitney Eichenger, Chris Rosselli, Robert Kallam, Michelle Peluso, Sam Gilliland, John Samuel, Scott Beckett, William Bratton, Terry Maxon, James Thompson, Julie Smith, Rick DeLisi, Maril Gagen MacDonald, Lindsay Thiele, Ron Williams, and John Dalton.

I thank everyone who helped along the way, whether mentioned here or not.

References

I've made these references more descriptive so you can understand whether a reference might be worth reading or contacting. I hope this helps.

INTRODUCTION

Change is constant. Gartner reports that the typical organization has undertaken five firmwide changes in the past three years. "Managing Organizational Change: Learn how HR can deliver on complex change initiatives," Gartner, 2019, https://www.gartner.com/en/human-resources/insights/organizational-change-management.

Two-thirds of change efforts fail. This is from a July 2008 *McKinsey Quarterly* article, "Creating Organizational Transformations," which references a 2008 McKinsey & Company survey of 3,199 executives from varied industries and regions. The article states that only one-third of respondents said their organizations succeeded in their change efforts. Rather than assuming that the other two-thirds were total failures, I chose to state that they fail or fall far short of their goals.

Growing research on the importance of emotion in decision-making. This is a reference to the work of Antonio Damasio and his colleagues, as discussed in Chapter 6 of this book. Other reading on the subject: Nasir Naqvi, Baba Shiv, and Antoine Beehara, "The Role of Emotion in Decision Making, A Cognitive Neuroscience Perspective," *Current Directions in Psychological Science* (October 1, 2006), 260–264. See also George Loewenstein, and Jennifer S. Lerner, "The Role of Affect in Decision Making," *Handbook of Affective Sciences* (2003), 619–642.

Majority of failed changes result from management's failure to show support or employee resistance. Boris Ewenstein, Wesley Smith, and Ashvin Sologar, "Changing Change Management," *Featured Insights*, McKinsey & Company, July 2015, https://www.mckinsey.com/featured-insights/leadership/changing-change-management.

$3 trillion spent on change each year. This is, admittedly, a conservative estimate. The International Data Corporation (IDC) estimates that about $1.5 trillion is already spent annually on digital transformation alone worldwide, and this number will grow to about $2 trillion by 2022. Considering how much change is nondigital in nature—mergers and other structural changes, for starters, plus leadership transitions, cultural transformations, globalization efforts, etc.—I believe I have very safely underestimated how much is spent on change overall. The point is about how much I hope to save organizations from wasting. Even if the IDC numbers were inflated, the amount of waste-minimization opportunity would still be massive. "Worldwide Spending on Digital Transformation Will Be Nearly $2 Trillion in 2022 as Organizations Commit to DX, According to a New IDC Spending Guide," IDC press release, November 13, 2018.

CHAPTER 1

Senses influence emotions. In addition to drawing on my own experiences and those of William Bratton in Chapter 7 of this book, I did general reading on the subject starting with a series of articles by Rebecca Rago, "Emotion and Our Senses," which ran in *Emotion on the Brain: The Neuroscience of Emotion, from Reaction to Regulation*, Department of Psychology, Tufts University, October–December 2014. From there, I was able to read and learn from numerous source articles.

CHAPTER 2

Cognitive dissonance. I've read about this theory many times through the years, and there are healthy debates among social psychology academics about what does and doesn't qualify as cognitive dissonance. For this book, I interviewed Skylar Brannon, an academic at the University of Texas at Austin, who is a chapter coauthor of the recently published *Cognitive Dissonance: Reexamining a Pivotal Theory in Psychology,* 2nd ed. (Washington, DC: American Psychological Association, 2019), which I also used for background source material.

Disk drive manufacturers. This information came from Clayton Christensen, *The Innovator's Dilemma*, (New York: HarperCollins, 1997), xv and 3–32. I've seen elsewhere that the life cycle of a fruit fly may be longer than a single day (actually as many as eight days), but Christensen says he learned this from a friend. Either way, the point is the same: it's much easier to study the generational genetics of fruit flies than that of people.

Michelle Peluso and Travelocity. I collaborated with Michelle Peluso on this story. The book referenced is Christopher W. L. Hart, *Extraordinary Guarantees: A New Way to Build Quality Throughout Your Company and Ensure Satisfaction for Your Customers* (New York: Amacom, 1993).

There wasn't room for it in the chapter, but—to elaborate

on this—Michelle and her team did a lot of very smart work in the twenty-four hours between becoming aware of the fare and the announcement that Travelocity would honor it. Understanding that this news story would be a boon for tourism to Fiji, they negotiated run-of-site banner advertising with the Fijian tourism authorities and other promotions with the country's hotel association. This helped to offset the cost of honoring the fare, but it was still a gamble, given that we had no idea how many people would actually take the flight. Some number didn't. It was no surprise that Michelle and her team found smart solutions quickly. Michelle is one of the smartest (IQ and EQ) people I've worked with, and she surrounded herself with people equally gifted in both quotients.

Tony Hsieh quote. This was told to me by Erica Javellana, who holds the title of Speaker of the House at Zappos during the Unstoppable Cultures Fellowship in November 2019.

CHAPTER 3

Overcommunicate. The quote about how communications should be "dripping from the walls" of your organization came during an interview with Scott Beckett of Insigniam. I first met Scott when he and the Insigniam team worked diligently and truly changed the managers of a Sabre subsidiary to the point where the division's frontline employees were commenting robustly about this change.

The story about the CEO thinking he had communicated heavily while his subordinates thought he was almost absent, as well as the rule of thumb to communicate three times more than you think you should came from Harold L. Kirklin, Perry Keenan, and Alan Jackson, "The Hard Side of Change Management," *Harvard Business Review* 83, no. 10 (October 2005): 108–118.

The estimate that some organizations only communicate 10 percent as much as they should came from John Kotter, "Leading Change," *Harvard Business Review* 85, no. 1 (March 1995): 96–103. Kotter said companies undercommunicate "by a factor of 10."

McKinsey & Company on best tactics among successful organizations. This came from the article "Creating organizational transformations," *McKinsey Quarterly* (July 2008), 9.

Communications is 90 percent action, 10 percent words. "Prove It with Action," "The Page Principles," Arthur W. Page Society, Page.org.

The Authentic Enterprise. The Authentic Enterprise, Arthur W. Page Society, page.org.

Furniture executive story. I learned about this from a friend who had heard the leader tell this story during a customer meeting. I spoke with an official at the company who confirmed the story, but for some reason, I couldn't get the company's permission to name them, so I left their name out.

Arthur Page writings on actions versus words. This was from a speech from the Bell System Executive Conference Talk, Asbury Park, N.J., November 1, 1955. https://bellisario.psu.edu/page-center/speech/bell-systems-executive-conference-talk

Franklin quote. Richard Saunders (aka Benjamin Franklin), *Poor Richard's Almanack* (Philadelphia, 1749). I've seen the word "show" written as "shew," which is an old spelling of the word.

References to Arthur Page Society. *The Authentic Enterprise*, The Arthur W. Page Society, page.org; and Roger Bolton, Don. W. Stacks and Eliot Mizrachi, eds., *The New Era of the CCO* (New York: Business Expert Press, 2018), page.org.

Sidebar on Gandhi. I first learned about this discrepancy from a *Washington Post* article: "Misquoting Einstein, Jefferson and Gandhi: A New Study Finds Members of Congress Can't Resist," *Washington Post*, May 17, 2019. This eventually led me to the link—active as of this writing—from Quote Investigator, https://quoteinvestigator.com/2017/10/23/be-change/, which is my end-all reference point.

CHAPTER 4

Other stuff gets in the way. The information about the hormonal response to stress comes from "Understanding the Stress Response," *Harvard Health Publishing*, May 1, 2018, https://www.health.harvard.edu/staying-healthy/understanding-the-stress-response.

Change fatigue. This information was provided by Maril MacDonald, CEO at Gagen MacDonald. The firm surveyed participants at a Conference Board Transformation Conference, where leaders said that "navigating change fatigue" was their most common frustration when driving change; 51.25 percent selected this response. This was a targeted survey of 86 people.

Energy slumps. It's more common than many realize, according to Bain & Company's "Transformation Catalyst," as told by Ivan Hindshaw, partner at Bain's Results Delivery Practice, in the accompanying video: https://www.bain.com/consulting-services/change-management-results-delivery/transformation-catalyst/.

Urgent/important matrix. This can be attributed to at least Eisenhower, for starters. I've seen many self-made matrices based on his matrix. Because I first learned about it through Stephen Covey, I'll reference his book *The 7 Habits of Highly Effective People*, (New York: Free Press, 1989), 149–162.

Deep Work. Cal Newport, *Deep Work: Rules for Focused Success in a Distracted World* (New York: Grand Central Publishing, 2016).

Getting Things Done. David Allen, *Getting Things Done: The Art of Stress-Free Productivity* (New York: Penguin Press, 2001).

A Sense of Urgency. John P. Kotter, *A Sense of Urgency* (Brighton, MA: Harvard Business School Press, 2008).

CHAPTER 5

Don't mess with Texas. Most people still are surprised to learn the origins of this message. For this book, the information came from Roy M. Spence Jr. and Haley Rushing, *It's Not What You Sell, It's What You Stand For* (New York: Penguin, 2009), 19–21.

The information about decreases in Texas littering from 2009 to 2013 came from a Texas Department of Transportation press release, "Don't Mess with Texas Leads to Reduction in Roadside Trash," September 3, 2013.

Forced compliance theory. Leon Festinger and James M. Carlsmith, "Cognitive Consequences of Forced Compliance," *Journal of Abnormal and Social Psychology* (58, no. 2, 1959), 203–210.

Purpose. Spence and Rushing, *It's Not What You Sell*, 9–11.

Story on continuous learning. I became aware of this story when interviewing Rick DeLisi, vice president and fellow at Gartner. At Rick's request, I have kept the company's identity confidential.

CHAPTER 6

Obama campaign. David Plouffe, *The Audacity to Win: The Inside Story and Lessons of Barack Obama's Historic Victory* (New York: Viking Press, 2009), 37–38 and 84–85.

Damasio and neuroscience. For this section, I relied heavily and took quotes from an interview between David Brooks, columnist for the *New York Times*, and Antonio Damasio during an Aspen Institute Ideas Festival in 2009. "This Time with Feeling: David Brooks and Antonio Damasio," Aspen Institute, January 29, 2015, YouTube video: 1:05:35, https://www.youtube.com/watch?v=IifXMd26gWE.

Descartes' Error. Antonio Damasio, *Descartes' Error: Emotion, Reason, and the Human Brain* (New York, HarperCollins, 1994).

CHAPTER 7

Good to Great. What would a business book be without at least one reference to this great book? Jim Collins, *Good to Great: Why Some Companies Make the Leap...and Others Don't* (New York: HarperCollins, 2001), 41.

Ron Williams and Aetna. Ron shared his regret about not making personnel decisions quickly during a leadership forum sponsored by the Arthur Page Society. His great book, which discusses the transformation in more depth, is *Learning to Lead: The Journey to Leading Yourself, Leading Others and Leading an Organization* (Austin, TX: Greenleaf Book Group, 2019).

Marsha Clark. For more information on Marsha, visit MarshaClarkandAssociates.com.

Tipping point. I came upon this—as it relates specifically to change management—by reading W. Chan Kim and Renee Mauborgne, "Tipping Point Leadership," *Harvard Business Review* 81, no. 4 (October 2003): 60–69.

William Bratton story. I interviewed William Bratton for this book. I first learned of Bratton's subway story from the "Tipping Point Leadership" article by Kim and Mauborgne. I learned more from William Bratton in his book *Turnaround: How America's Top Cop Reversed the Crime Epidemic* (New York: Random House, 1998), 143–164.

Subway crime rates. Emma G. Fitzsimmons and Edgar

Sandoval, "New York Tackled Subway Crime, but Is It Coming Back?" *New York Times*, February 4, 2019. This article states that violent crime fell from approximately 17,500 crimes in 1990, when there were one billion riders, to 2,500 crimes in 2018, when there were 1.7 billion riders. The article mentions that crime rates tipped up slightly in 2018. In our interview, Bratton mentioned statistics showing a similar drop for all crime—not just violent crime—during the same period.

CHAPTER 8

Push-pull leadership. While I came to this idea independently, it turns out, push-pull leadership is a thing. From what I can tell, it's a small thing, not even a cottage-industry-sized thing, but there are a few people who have talked about this concept over the years. Here is an early explanation of this somewhat similar concept to mine: Stever Robbins, "The 'Pull Leadership' Manifesto," *Working Knowledge*, Havard Business School, August 23, 2004, https://hbswk.hbs.edu/archive/the-pull-leadership-manifesto.

Dan Gilbert story. The 1998 email to employees was featured in *Isms in Action* (Detroit: Quicken Loans, 2015). Isms are the values held by Gilbert's family of companies. I confirmed other insights about Quicken and Gilbert with Whitney Eichinger, an official at Gilbert's holding company.

Unfortunately, Gilbert was recovering from a stroke during my writing, so I was unable to interview him.

CHAPTER 10

Eighty percent of companies use a top-down change management approach. Marcus Chiu, and Heather Salerno, "Changing Change Management: An Open-Source Approach," Gartner, 2019, https://www.gartner.com/en/human-resources/trends/changing-change-management. I also interviewed Rick DeLisi, vice president and fellow at Gartner, for this book.

"Understanding Change" chart. Salerno, "Changing Change Management."

IBM jams. This was told to me by Jon Iwata, former senior vice president, marketing and communications, IBM.

Pixar Notes Day. This came from Ed Catmull, *Creativity, Inc.: Overcoming the Unseen Forces That Stand in the Way of True Inspiration* (New York: Random House, 2014), 275–295.

You get the brain for free. The quote, "When you buy a pair of hands, you get the brain for free," came from a speech I helped write in 1989 for Geoff Zeh when he was president of the Brotherhood of Maintenance of Way Employes. Geoff provided this line to us; it's his.

Successful organizations are four times as likely to include fifty-plus people in planning change. Scott Keller, Mary Meaney, and Caroline Pung, "What Successful Transformations Share: March 2010 Survey," McKinsey & Company, https://www.mckinsey.com/business-functions/organization/our-insights/what-successful-transformations-share-mckinsey-global-survey-results. McKinsey says 25 percent of organizations that were "extremely successful" in their change efforts included groups of fifty or more, while only 6 percent of unsuccessful organizations did so.

CHAPTER 11

SabreTown story. I collaborated with Sam Gilliland and John Samuel for this story.

About the Author

AL COMEAUX, a former executive at Travelocity, GE and American Airlines, is a decorated corporate pioneer and global authority on change from inside organizations. His career championing change as a senior leader at uber-disruptive dot-coms as well as established, world-renowned companies—and his twenty-year journey researching why so many change efforts fail and what's needed for success—make him one of the world's most forward thinkers on what leaders must do—and how they must think—to succeed at change.

In 2019, Al founded Primed for Change, a disruptive new project created to prepare leaders to take organizations successfully through change. Al and his family live in Ft. Worth, Texas, where he is deeply involved in his family, faith, and community.

Index

A

actions (vs. words), 30, 52, 74–76, 79, 85, 86, 233, 240, 255
Aetna, 155, 259
agile development, 38–40, 219, 222, 226
Allen, David, 112, 257
American Airlines, 10, 18, 211, 263
amount spent/wasted on change, 26, 250–251
amygdala, 142, 245
Arthur W. Page Society (Page), 80–82, 91, 254–55, 259
Aspen Institute Ideas Festival, 258
AT&T, 85
Audacity to Win, The, 137, 258
Authentic Enterprise, The, 82, 91, 254, 255

B

Bain & Company, 107, 256
Bartlett's Familiar Quotations, 93
Beckett, Scott, 247, 253
Beethoven's Fifth Symphony, 198
Bezos, Jeff, 114
Boston Consulting Group, 211
Boston Police Department, 161
Brannon, Skylar, 252
Bratton, William, 160–65, 174, 218, 251, 259–60
broken windows theory, 161
Brooks, David, 258
Brotherhood of Maintenance of Way Employees, 261

C

Catmull, Ed, 261

change agents, 10, 41, 229

change by decree, 117–33, 216, 240

change context, 216–226, 237, 241

change management, 10, 13–23, 31–35, 73, 87, 90–95, 107, 139, 144, 147, 180, 223, 237, 259, 261

Christensen, Clayton, 52–55, 252

Clark, Marsha, 155, 259

Cleveland Cavaliers, 179–80

Cleveland Clinic, 66

Clinton, Hillary, campaign, 137–38

cognitive dissonance, 49–69, 88, 90, 92, 157–58, 191, 252

Cognitive Dissonance: Reexamining a Pivotal Theory in Psychology, 252

Cohen, Dan, 44

Collins, Jim, 154, 259

Conference Board Transformation Conference, 256

consonance, 193–96

continuous learning story, 129–30, 174, 258

controlling the message, 209, 213

core values, values, 16, 104, 112–133, 148, 154, 202, 216–23, 225, 237, 240–41, 260

cortisol and stress, 100

Covey, Stephen, 21, 108, 256

Creativity, Inc., 261

culture, 11, 64, 85, 121, 140, 182

Current Directions in Psychological Science, 250

D

Damasio, Antonio, 142–44, 250, 258

Deep Work, 111–12, 257

DeLisi, Rick, 258, 261

Descartes' Error, 143, 258

desktop personal computer industry, 54

Diary of a Young Girl, The, 65

Dilbert, 122

disk drive industry, 52–55, 252

disruption, 12, 18, 31, 176–80

Disruption OFF, 12

disruptive innovation, principles of, 55

Don't Mess With Texas campaign, 117–20, 257

E

EDS, 155

Eichinger, Whitney, 260

Eisenhower, Dwight, 108, 256

Emerson, Ralph Waldo, 85

Emotion on the Brain: The Neuroscience of Emotion, from Reaction to Regulation, 251
emotions and change, 19, 142-47
Extraordinary Guarantees, 19, 252

F

Facebook, 230
fatigue, related to change, 106-07, 256
Festinger, Leon, 50, 257
fight or flight, 100
Fiji
    $1 fare to, 57-58, 218, 253
    Fiji Airways, 62
forced compliance theory, 126, 131, 257
Fortune, 135
Fox News, 49-50
Frank, Anne, 65
Franklin, Benjamin, 85, 255
furniture manufacturer story, 82-85, 174, 218, 232, 254

G

Gagen MacDonald, 106, 256
Gandhi, 93, 255
Gartner, 206, 210, 249, 258, 261
GE, 18, 66, 102, 263
    GE Aviation, 211
GEICO, 74, 199-200
Getting Things Done, 112, 257
Gilbert, Dan (Daniel), 177-82, 184, 206, 218, 260-61
Gilliland, Sam, 230-34, 262
Glassdoor.com, 39, 81
Good to Great, 154, 258-59
GSD&M ad agency, 118

H

Handbook of Affective Sciences, 250
harmony, 105, 196-203
Harvard Business Review, 254, 259
Harvard Business School, *Working Knowledge,* 260
Harvard Health Publishing, 256
Have a backbone, disagree and commit, 88, 114
heart, 18-22, 106, 142-50, 240-42
    and SMART, 18-19, 141-51, 240, 242
Heart of Change, The, 44
Hindshaw, Ivan, 256
Hsieh, Tony, 65, 253

I

IBM, 53

Jams, 212, 261

Indeed.com, 39

inertia, 95–115, 187, 240

Inferno, 162

influencers, seeding information to, 234

Innovator's Dilemma, The, 52, 252

inputs vs outcomes, 19, 138–51

Insigniam, 73, 253

intellect vs heart (or emotion), 19–20, 146, 241, 242

International Data Corporation (IDC), 250–51

isms and *Isms in Action,* 182, 260

It's Not What You Sell, It's What You Stand For, 128, 257

Iwata, John, 261

J

Javellana, Erica, 253

Jones, Terry, 9–12

Journal of Abnormal and Social Psychology, 257

K

Kayak, 12

Kennedy, John F., 85

Kotter, John, 44, 112, 254, 257

KPIs, 139–40, 145–46

L

Lanier, Bob, 119

laptop industry, 55

Learning to Lead, 259

Lee, Harper, 65

LinkedIn, 39

listening, 20, 47, 147, 207–12, 223

London Olympics of 1920, 170

Lorrance, Arlene, 93

Los Angeles Police Department, 160

Love Project, The, 93

M

mainframe industry, 53–54

Marketplace, 49

McKinsey & Company, 16, 25, 79, 208, 250, 254

Featured Insights, 249
  McKinsey Quarterly, 249, 254
Microtrends, 138
Millennium Hotels, 232
mindfulness, 66
minicomputer industry, 53
modeling change, 15, 20, 23, 24, 37, 46, 47, 56, 63, 84, 85, 88, 89, 92, 103, 112, 114, 128-29, 142, 151, 154, 158, 163-66, 183, 220-21, 228, 234, 237
moon shot, the, 200
MSNBC, 50
Myspace, 230

N

neuroscience, 142, 250, 258
New Era of the CCO, The, 91, 255
New York Police Department, 160-61
New York subway system, 161-65, 259-60
New York Times, 258, 260
New York Transit Police Department, 161, 164, 174
Newport, Cal, 111, 257

O

Obama campaign, 137-39, 258
Office, The, 132
Office Space, 122-23, 131
ON Innovation, 12
open-source change, 210, 261

P

Page, Arthur W., 85, 255
Page Principles, 80, 254
Peluso, Michelle, 57-64, 173, 218, 252
Penn, Mark, 138
Pixar, 212-13
    Notes Day, 212, 261
Plouffe, David, 137-38, 258
Poor Richard's Almanack, 255
primed for change, 139, 173, 242
Principle-Centered Leadership, 21
public radio, 49
pulling (for change), 20, 47, 142, 154, 170-84, 206-07
purpose, 127-28, 211-12, 258
Purpose Institute, The, 212
push vs pull, 154, 169-86, 206, 241, 260

Q

Quicken Loans, 179–80, 206, 260
Quote Investigator, 93, 255

R

Railway Labor Act, 193
rational connection, 20
Rock Financial, 177–81
rumor mill, 209
Rushing, Haley, 257
Ryssdal, Kai, 49

S

Sabre, 10, 18, 230–34, 253, 262
    SabreTown, 232–34, 262
Samuel, John, 231, 262
Saturday Night Live, 74
Saunders, Richard (aka Benjamin Franklin), 255
Sense of Urgency, A, 112, 257
7 Habits of Highly Effective People, The, 21, 108, 109, 113, 256
Shawshank Redemption, 124
SMART, 18–19, 141, 142, 144–45, 148–51, 240, 242
    and heart, 18–19, 141–51, 240, 242
social networking, 230–33
social psychology, 50, 126, 252, 257
Spence, Roy Jr., 128, 212, 257, 258
Stegner, John, 44–46, 160
storytelling, power of, 72–73, 159
symphony, 196–201
synchrony, 241

T

Texas Highway Commission, 118
Texas litter problem, 117–20, 174, 257
tipping point change, 160–61
Tipping Point Leadership, 259
To Kill a Mockingbird, 65
top-down change, 123–24, 180, 206, 210, 223, 261
Travelocity, 10, 12, 18, 31, 57–63, 173, 218, 252
    customer championship, 61–62, 173, 218, 228
    customer guarantee, 59–65
Tufts University, Department of Psychology, 251
Turnaround, 259
Twitter, 170, 229

U

unison, 198–203
United Airlines, 58
University of Iowa, 142
University of Minnesota, 50
University of Southern California, 143
University of Texas at Austin, 252
Unstoppable Cultures Fellowship, 253
Urgent/Important Matrix, 108-13, 256
us-*versus*-them feeling, 209

V

values. *see* core values, values
variation, 200–01

W

want to change, 13, 20, 26, 39–40, 43, 66, 76, 91, 105, 107, 121, 126, 133, 140, 149, 150, 151, 153, 154, 173, 213, 239, 242
Washington Post, 255
waterfall development, 38–40
"*we*" problem vs. "*they*" problem, 29-46, 48
When you buy a pair of hands, you get the brain for free, 213, 261
Williams, Ron, 155, 259
World War II, 108

Y

Y2K effort, 123

Z

Zappos, 65, 253
Zeh, Geoff, 261
ZipRecruiter, 39

CPSIA information can be obtained
at www.ICGtesting.com
Printed in the USA
FSHW022044150520

9 781544 509150